The Cradle of Maryland Horse Racing

KIMBERLY GATTO

To Sue & Dick –
I hope you enjoy
this book!
All the best,
Kim Gatto

Charleston · London

THE
History
PRESS

Published by The History Press
Charleston, SC 29403
www.historypress.net

Front cover, Nashua wins over Summer Tan in the 1955 Wood Memorial, 16" x 12" acrylic
painting by Theresa Aresco of Photofinishstudio.com.
Back cover, top, courtesy of Belair Stable Museum; bottom, courtesy of Louise Ferro Martin.

Cover design by Natasha Walsh.

First published 2012

Manufactured in the United States

ISBN 978.1.60949.481.0

Library of Congress CIP data applied for.

*In loving memory of Chutney
(1977–2008),
whose great resemblance to her grandsire,
Nashua,
first sparked my interest in Belair Stud.*

Contents

Foreword, by Pam Williams and Russ Davies
   of the Belair Stable Museum   7
Acknowledgements   9

1. Origins of Belair   11
2. Tasker's Selima   15
3. The Taskers and the Ogles   21
4. The Early Woodward Era   25
5. William Woodward, Master of Belair   31
6. The Roaring Twenties   39
7. The Fox of Belair   47
8. Omaha, the Belair Bullet   59
9. Other Belair Favorites   67
10. A Changing of the Guards   81
11. Nashua the Great   85
12. Triumph and Tragedy   95
13. Belair Lives On   105

Appendix A. Offspring of Selima   111
Appendix B. Pedigrees of Key Belair Horses   113
Appendix C. Racing Records of Key Belair Stud Champions   119
Appendix D. Winners of Key Races Named for Belair or Its Horses   127
Notes   153
Index   157
About the Author   160

FOREWORD

On March 30, 1737, the Reverend Jacob Henderson sold three parcels of land for £500 to Benjamin Tasker Sr. and Governor Samuel Ogle. Those parcels included Woodcock's Range, Enfield Chase and Belair. Thus began Belair's long and colorful history—one closely intertwined with the history of the American Thoroughbred horse.

Belair Plantation, later Belair Stud Stable, is like all ancient homeplaces. The mansion and stable—museums today—are filled with the echoes of laughter and tears, hopes and joys, successes and failures of all the individuals who lived and worked here. The story of Belair is rich. It is a story of the Thoroughbred and the men who owned them, trained them, loved them and, most importantly, respected them. The lives of many of them—slave and free, black and white—were lives spent in the care and training of these magnificent animals.

In the eighteenth century, Samuel Ogle and his brother-in-law, Colonel Benjamin Tasker—with the importation of bloodstock like Selima, Spark and Queen Mab—gave cause for Belair Plantation to become the "Cradle of American Thoroughbred Racing." In the twentieth century, noted American horseman William Woodward developed a stable at Belair that was internationally famous. Woodward racers like Gallant Fox, Omaha and Nashua followed in the hoofbeats of those eighteenth-century legends, becoming legends in their own right.

In 1957, after a two-hundred-year adventure in Thoroughbred racing, Belair Stud and Farm was sold to developer William J. Levitt. Today, museums interpret Belair's role in racing and commemorate the lives of all its residents. A housing development, with streets named after Gallant Fox and Nashua, covers the fields where some of America's best Thoroughbreds roamed and grazed. But the contribution of Belair to racing history will never be forgotten. Thank you to Kimberly Gatto for telling our story. Winston Churchill wrote: "There is something about the outside of a horse that is good for the inside of a man." Ms. Gatto's publication, and the history it records, is good for the inside of all of us.

Pam Williams, Museums Manager—City of Bowie Museums
Russ Davies, Stable Facility Manager—City of Bowie Museums
January 2012

ACKNOWLEDGEMENTS

The author would like to thank the following individuals for helping to make this work possible:

Pam Williams and Russ Davies Sr. of the Belair Stable Museum for contributing their vast knowledge, providing key insight and support and allowing me to use the photographs from the museum's archives. Their contributions have been immense;

The City of Bowie for its continuing dedication to the acknowledgement and preservation of its history and that of Thoroughbred racing history;

Allison Pareis for reviewing the manuscript and assisting with photographs, providing support and valuable feedback and always being there with a kind word of friendship;

Louise Ferro Martin for traveling to Belair to take photographs and offering valuable support;

Theresa Aresco, Heather Rohde and William Wilson for allowing me to use their wonderful artwork;

Cindy and Tex Dulay, Jessie Holmes and Cheryl Denton for allowing me to use their fabulous photographs;

Chris Poole for stepping in to take photographs and doing such a wonderful job;

Hannah Cassilly of The History Press for her patience throughout the project;

Patrick Lennon for his careful review of the manuscript, as well as continued support and friendship;

Michael Blowen, Vivien Morrison, Susan Salk, Beth McDonald and Margaret Schubert for support and feedback throughout the writing process;

All my family and friends for their unending support, and especially my mom, Ann Urquhart, for always believing in me; and

My late mare, Chutney, and my current horse, Grace, for showing me that there truly is no horse quite as lovely as a Thoroughbred.

Chapter 1

ORIGINS OF BELAIR

Centuries before Nashua first set foot on a racetrack, the estate now known as Belair was established in Collington, Prince Georges County, Maryland (now known as Bowie). The parcel, measuring five hundred acres and bearing the early name of Catton, was situated within the heart of Maryland's tobacco farming area. It was patented in 1681 by the Calvert family, the first proprietors of the Maryland Colony, for a man by the name of Robert Carvile. An attorney by trade, Carvile was far too engrossed in his legal practice to spend much time developing the property. In 1698, he sold Catton to Colonel Henry Ridgely for the sum of £100.

Over the next few years, Ridgely made various improvements to the property, including the construction of a house, various outbuildings, an arbor and a barn. Colonel Ridgely operated Catton as a plantation with the assistance of about thirty-two slaves. When Ridgely passed away in 1699, the property was bequeathed to his wife, Mary. Several years later, Mary Ridgely married the Reverend Jacob Henderson, rector of Maryland's Queen Anne Parish.

As owner of Catton, Henderson had reason to believe that others were trespassing on the property and petitioned the land office to resurvey its boundaries. The new survey estimated the land at 1,410 acres—nearly three times the size of its original tract. When a new deed was issued in 1721, the property was given the name of Belair.

In 1731, British cavalry captain Samuel Ogle was appointed provincial governor of Maryland by Charles Calvert, fifth baron of Baltimore, and dispatched to colonial America. Ogle, the son of a prominent family, was born in 1694 in Northumberland, England. In early October 1731, Ogle boarded a ship from his homeland for the rough two-month journey to Annapolis.

As part of his compensation as governor, Ogle was granted £3,000 to establish a residence in the new colony. After several years as a bachelor, Ogle decided to purchase the land on which he would build a home. In March 1737, he partnered with a friend, Benjamin Tasker Sr., to purchase Henderson's Belair property. The price was of the land was £500, with each man contributing half of the total. Several months after the purchase, Ogle purchased Tasker's share of the property, thereby becoming the sole owner of the Belair estate.

Tasker and Ogle had much in common. Tasker was the son of an Englishman and, like Ogle, maintained considerable wealth and a prominent social standing. A successful businessman, Tasker was one of the founders of the Baltimore Ironworks Company. He would hold several colonial offices over the years, including mayor of Annapolis, and would later serve as proprietary governor of Maryland.

The two men also shared an appreciation for fine horses. According to sources, Samuel Ogle was instrumental in the early breeding of English blooded horses in America. He imported several Spanish Barb mares to the new colony and, as early as the year 1735, had sent one such mare to Virginia to be bred to the stallion Bulle Rock.[1] In the years to follow, Ogle would become the owner of several racehorses and would later be credited with the establishment of the Annapolis Subscription Plate, the oldest formal recorded horse race in Maryland.

In 1741, the families of Ogle and Tasker were officially joined by marriage. In a union that likely raised eyebrows at the time, Governor Ogle, at the age of forty-seven, married Tasker's eighteen-year-old daughter, Anne. Known affectionately as "Nancy," the lovely Anne Tasker was "a much sought-after belle."[2] She was gifted not only with beauty and style but also with intelligence and sophistication. Anne, unlike many women of colonial days, was able to read and express herself in writing.

Less than a year after the nuptials, Ogle's term as governor ended. Another Maryland resident, Thomas Bladen, had married into the family of Lord Baltimore and, in an example of nepotism, was appointed the new governor. With his term as governor completed, Ogle and his wife packed up their belongings and boarded a ship for a stint in England. Upon departure, Ogle left Tasker in charge of the Belair property, with instructions to construct a home on the purchased land.

While the Ogles were in England, Tasker oversaw the construction of the Belair mansion—"the grandest [home] in the region" with "a magnificent, all-encompassing view of the plantation."[3] As labor was scarce at that time, the mansion took several years to construct. The home, a Georgian-style brick mansion, was situated on an incline, with windows on all sides to allow the sun to pervade the rooms. The sprawling property boasted gardens with terraces, a greenhouse, a deer park and various other buildings. When the Ogles returned to Maryland in 1747, they took residence of the grand estate.

Ogle operated Belair as a full plantation and kept numerous animals on its vast acreage. In addition to horses, Belair housed an assortment of other species, including cattle, hogs, oxen, sheep, fowl and, at one point, a buffalo. In order to properly care for the animals, Ogle hired a young man by the name of Jacob Green to oversee the stables and plantation.

Also in residence at Ogle's Belair were two prized English Thoroughbreds. These horses, a stallion called Spark and a mare named Queen Mab, were gifts to Ogle from England's Lord Baltimore. Spark was foaled in 1743 and had originally been presented to Frederick, Prince of Wales. He was sired by Aleppo (from the line of the Darley Arabian) out of a mare called Miss Colvill. Also of royal lineage, Queen Mab was bred by Thomas Smith and foaled at the Royal Stud at Hampton Court in England. Spark and Queen Mab were the first English Thoroughbreds to be imported into Maryland.

The arrival of Queen Mab and Spark at Belair was instrumental in the early development of the American Thoroughbred racehorse. In the years to come, these horses would establish the bloodlines that would propel Belair into the "Cradle of Thoroughbred Racing" in America.

Chapter 2
TASKER'S SELIMA

In May 1752, Maryland mourned the death of Governor Samuel Ogle. After a lengthy illness, Ogle passed away at his home in Annapolis, leaving behind his wife, Anne Tasker, and the couple's three young children. The bulk of Ogle's estate, including the Belair property, was bequeathed to his three-year-old son, Benjamin. Due to the child's age, the governor's will named his wife's brother (and Tasker's son), Colonel Benjamin Tasker Jr., as interim manager of the Belair estate.

Colonel Tasker, at age thirty-two, had already gained prominent political and social standing in the community. He was also a noted horseman who was engaged in the breeding of Thoroughbred racing bloodstock. Colonel Tasker began his breeding efforts by mating Spark with Belair's Spanish mares but quickly determined his preference for the more elegant English bloodlines. Author Fairfax Harrison wrote in his 1929 book, *The Belair Stud*, "Colonel Tasker was the first in Maryland to learn the lesson that if one is to breed at all it is worthwhile only to breed 'true' and from the best."[4]

Tasker evidently had an eye for "the best," as was proven when he imported the mare Selima in the fall of 1750. Foaled on April 30, 1745, Selima was a daughter of the Godolphin Arabian out of Shireborn, a mare from the personal stable of Queen Anne. The Godolphin Arabian was one of the original three foundation stallions (along with the Darley Arabian and the Byerly Turk) who created the Thoroughbred as a breed. Also known as the Godolphin Barb, the striking "gold touched" bay was foaled in 1724, likely in Yemen or Tunisia, and was shipped to France to the stable of King Louis XIV. The horse was purchased in Paris by Englishman Edward Coke, who shipped the animal to his homeland in 1729. After Coke's death, the Arabian was sold to Francis Leonard, Second Earl of Godolphin, from whom the horse would derive its name. A prominent breeder, Godolphin owned a farm near Newmarket, the premier horse-racing area in England.

According to legend, the Godolphin Arabian was originally thought too small to be a breeding stud. However, when a broodmare by the name of Lady Roxana rejected her proposed mate, she was covered by Godolphin's bay stallion. The results were impressive, as the foal of this mating, Lath, became the greatest racer of his day. The second breeding of Lady Roxana with the Godolphin Arabian produced Cade, a five-time leading sire in Great Britain and Ireland. Regulus, another colt sired by the Godolphin Arabian, was undefeated on the track and led the aforementioned sire list for a period of eight years. With such exceptional offspring credited to his name, the Godolphin Arabian was recognized as a leading racehorse stallion and would be bred only to the finest mares.

The veterinary surgeon William Osmer, as quoted by historian C.M. Prior, described the Godolphin Arabian as follows:

> *There never was a horse (at least, that I have seen) so well entitled to get racers as the Godolphin Arabian; for, whoever has seen this horse must remember that his shoulders were deeper, and lay farther into his back, than those of any horse ever yet seen. Behind the shoulders, there was but a very small space ere the muscles of his loins rose exceedingly high, broad, and expanded, which were inserted into his hindquarters with greater strength and power than in any horse I believe ever yet seen of his dimensions, viz fifteen hands high.*[5]

Stamped with the stunning good looks of her sire, Selima was a lovely bay with a symmetrical star and a white hind coronet. The mare caught the eye of Colonel Tasker, who was completing an English tour of duty in September 1750. Impressed by the mare's attractive conformation, Tasker purchased Selima for an unknown sum and shipped her to the Belair farm. Records allege that Selima was in foal when she was purchased by Tasker; however, there is no record of any offspring born to her at that time. It is assumed that the foal was aborted or died during the long and tenuous journey overseas.

After arriving safely at Belair, Selima was trained for Tasker and made her racing debut at Annapolis in May 1752. There she defeated another English mare, Creeping Kate, and earned a purse of fifty Spanish gold coins (known as pistoles) for Belair Stud.

Around the time that Selima was training at Belair, a young Virginian named William Byrd III spent his days boasting about his wealth. Byrd's father and grandfather had made a fortune in the fur trade business, which left young William with more money than he could handle. Byrd fit the caricature of a proverbial showoff who enjoyed singing his own praises to anybody who would listen. The young man was also a reckless gambler who was notorious for making frivolous bets. On one occasion, Byrd lost thousands of English pounds in a single card game while playing against the Royal Duke of Cumberland.

By 1752, Thoroughbred races were becoming increasingly popular in Virginia and its surrounding areas. In response, Byrd—who was unable to resist gambling of any sort or kind—opted to give the prestigious "sport of kings" a try. In his estimation, success would be easy; all he would need was an appropriate horse. As was characteristic of Byrd, he did not give the acquisition much thought. Soon he had purchased Tryal, a ten-year-old chestnut Thoroughbred—a horse without any racing history.

When the horse arrived on the ship from England, Byrd could barely wait to show off his new purchase. He made a bold decree, challenging any horse owner who dared to face Tryal in a race. With money as no object, Byrd offered up a hefty purse of 500 Spanish pistoles—enough, according to *Smithsonian* magazine, to "furnish a mansion or buy a dozen slaves."[6] The race was to be a winner-take-all duel over four miles near the Williamsburg colony.

With such a large sum of money at stake, several prominent horse breeders responded to Byrd's call. Colonel Francis Thornton of Virginia would enter an unnamed gray mare. Breeder John Tayloe II, also from Virginia, would bring two imported Thoroughbreds, Childers and Jenny Cameron. And Colonel Tasker of Belair would cross state lines to enter Selima. With five horses entered at 500 pistoles apiece, the winner's purse was the largest for any horse race at that time.

The race took place on December 5, 1752, at Anderson's Race Ground in Gloucester, Virginia. Few specific details are known. According to sources, however, Selima would likely have walked 150 grueling miles to the Race Ground, as horses were not transported by cart at that time. The other horses also would have been hand-walked to the event but were housed within a few short miles of the destination. In the race, the horses would have carried approximately 140 pounds and were likely ridden by young African American slaves.

According to *Smithsonian*, "The only known newspaper account was a brief report in Annapolis' *Maryland Gazette* listing the order of finish and referring to the occasion as 'great.'" That order of finish was not in William Byrd's favor. Selima garnered her second win in as many starts, defeating Tryal and the others over Virginia's rough terrain. The finish was listed as Selima, Tryal, Thornton's mare and Tayloe's two imports, in that order, and the event was heralded as the first "major" horse race in the new colony.

William Byrd was disgusted. Not only did his Tryal fail to win the race, but Byrd had embarrassed himself and fellow Virginians by allowing a Maryland horse to defeat them. At that point, a decree was issued to ban all Maryland horses from competing in Virginia. Maryland breeders thwarted this rule by sending their mares out of state to deliver foals. For Byrd's part, while he continued to import horses, he never entered another race.

Following this epic victory, Selima began the next phase of her life as a broodmare at Belair Stud. There she produced six foals for Colonel Tasker. Among them was Selim, a handsome bay colt foaled in 1759. Known as "the terrible Selim" due to his difficult temperament, Selim was one of the most successful racehorses of his time. He made his debut at the age of four and was undefeated for five straight years, ultimately retiring at age thirteen with very few losses. Selim's most well-known race occurred in 1766, when he bested the equally famous Yorick, a Virginia-bred chestnut, for a purse of 100 pistoles.

What originated as a keen judgment by Colonel Tasker on a visit to England turned out to be a monumental development in the history of Thoroughbred racing. Selima was to become the foundation mare of the American Thoroughbred breed, with her early descendants including immortals such as Lexington, Foxhall and Hanover.

Selima's memory continues to live on in Maryland and throughout the entire horse-racing community. In her honor, the Selima Stakes for two-year-old fillies was established at Laurel Race Course in 1926. At the time of its origin at the Maryland State Fair, the race offered the richest purse for fillies at that time. Fittingly, the winner's trophy would be donated by Belair Stud (and William Woodward, owner at that time), with the following inscription: "This cup and cover is presented by the Belair Stud, in memory of Selima (by the Godolphin Arabian), imported to Belair in the reign of George the Second. Selima became the ancestress of Hanover, Foxhall, and many fine

The Selima plaque commissioned by William Woodward. *Courtesy of the Belair Stable Museum.*

racehorses." A plaque featuring a bronze likeness of the broodmare Selima would later be commissioned by Woodward; it would be affixed to the stable wall, further honoring Selima's place in the history of Belair.

Racing historian John Hervey wrote of Selima:

> *In Selima we behold one of those majestic matriarchs whose greatness is monumental. She was the queen of the turf in her day, and when sent to the stud disseminated an influence through a large family of both sexes that makes the history of her descendants synonymous with that of the American turf and breed of horses. A statement that might seem extravagant were it not in broad terms the truth.*[7]

Chapter 3

THE TASKERS AND
THE OGLES

With Selima settled into life as a broodmare, Colonel Tasker managed all aspects of the Belair estate. He also served as guardian and executor of the late governor's will and oversaw the education of young Benjamin Ogle. In the years following Governor Ogle's death, Anne and the children had moved back to Annapolis, leaving Colonel Tasker effectively serving as master of Belair. Tasker used this time wisely, making various improvements to the estate. According to historian Shirley Baltz, these enhancements included clearing "meadow ground…found and inclosed [*sic*] a large garden at very large expense…planted many pear trees, planted locust and poplar avenues to the house…inclosed with posts and rails a deer park, and converted some of the arable land into pasture by sowing the same with clover and other grass seeds."[8] Tasker also planted a grape vineyard from which wine "rare enough to achieve some degree of recognition" was produced.

Additionally, Tasker bolstered the Belair Stud breeding program by standing several prominent stallions. One of these was Othello, an attractive British Thoroughbred who had been imported to the United States in 1755. The stallion was described as a "beautiful black horse standing 15 hands tall" and was sometimes referred to as "Portmore's Othello" or "black and all black." Othello's mating with Selima produced several foals, including the aforementioned "terrible Selim." Othello's owner, Maryland governor Horatio Sharpe, was a friend of Tasker's and a frequent visitor to Belair.

Colonel Tasker's tenure as master of Belair was sadly much shorter than expected, as he died in 1760 at the age of thirty-nine. The task of operating Belair now reverted back to Benjamin Tasker Sr., who was left as executor of his son's will. Under its provisions, a public auction was held on May 21, 1761, during which thirty "blooded horses, mares and fillies" were offered for sale. The horses, valued at £710, included "the noted bay mare Selima, four of her foals, the breeding mare belonging to the late Governor Ogle, and their increase."[9] According to historian Baltz, these animals were Tasker's most valuable possessions. Selima was purchased by John Tayloe and shipped to his Mount Airy Stud in Virginia; there she lived out the remainder of her years, producing four foals, including the filly Black Selima.

Tasker Sr. would remain in charge of Belair until his death in 1768. He would also serve as guardian to young Benjamin Ogle, who had been sent to boarding school in England at the age of ten. Under the conditions of his late father's will, Benjamin Ogle could take possession of Belair upon reaching adulthood. In the meantime, after the death of Tasker Sr., the Belair property was occupied by various Tasker family members.

Having returned to Maryland as a young adult, Benjamin Ogle took possession of the Belair estate in 1774. During his reign as master of Belair, Ogle renovated the stables and made various other additions to the vast property. The estate in the Benjamin Ogle era boasted numerous structures, including a meat house, tobacco house and deer house. Due to its immense size and operation as a full plantation, Belair depended on the service of numerous slaves. Ogle employed a full staff to ensure that all areas of the estate continued to operate smoothly.

Like his father and uncle before him, Ogle was an avid owner of Thoroughbreds and often entered his horses in local events. Ogle's colt Oscar (by Gabriel) won several key races, including back-to-back runnings of both the Jockey Club Purse in Annapolis and the City Purse in Washington in 1804 and 1805, respectively. Oscar's wins during the following year included the Baltimore Jockey Club Purse. Ogle was also active in the Annapolis Jockey Club; when the club reorganized in March 1783, Ogle was named as one of its twenty-six original members. In later years, Ogle would become governor of Maryland, a position he would maintain from 1798 to 1801. He was also a friend to various politicians, including the first president of the United States. Records assert that George Washington often sought counsel from Ogle and dined at the Belair mansion on at least one occasion. In fact, Ogle is credited with the establishment of what is now regarded as President's Day, as he had proclaimed a day of mourning after the passing of his friend George Washington.

In the years preceding his death in 1809, Benjamin Ogle passed the Belair property on to his son, Benjamin II. Ogle II and his wife, Anna Maria, were the parents of fourteen growing children. As such, they were in need of a large dwelling, and the expansive Belair mansion was more than adequate for their needs. While previous owners had considered Belair an occasional or weekend retreat, it served as the primary residence for the family of Benjamin Ogle II.

With such a large family to support, Ogle II had little money to spend on the luxuries that previous Belair masters had enjoyed. The extravagance of horse breeding and racing was far beyond the family's means. Ogle II would operate the estate until his death several decades later, but Belair's long affiliation with horse racing came to an abrupt end. According to Baltz:

> The publication of the American Turf Register and Sporting magazine from 1829 into the mid-1830s stirred only memories of the earlier halcyon days at Belair. Racetracks had been flourishing in Baltimore and Washington since the first part of the century and the magazine reported current entries in, and results of, their races. In no instance did the Ogle name appear. Belair emerged only in letters to the editor furnishing bloodlines of ancient horses and tracing a number of them back to Ogle's Oscar, Othello, Col. Tasker's Selima, Selim, and even to Spark and Queen Mab.[10]

Ogle II passed away in 1844, leaving the Belair property to his sons, George and Richard Ogle. The two men divided the estate into separate parcels, with George taking ownership of the Belair mansion and Richard inhabiting a portion of the land known as Bladen. George's revision of the Belair deed included a rather unusual provision—his younger sister, Rosalie, could remain in the mansion for as long as she was unmarried.

The ratification of the state constitution of 1864 emancipated the slaves in Maryland and ended Belair's operation as a plantation. In 1867, George Ogle reported to the Maryland state commissioner that he had released forty-one slaves. Without such workers to maintain its operations, the property fell into severe disrepair. The Ogles struggled financially, garnering large debts and defaulting on at least one loan. In 1871, Belair was sold at auction, with the following description:

Belair's James T. Woodward. *Courtesy of the Belair Stable Museum.*

550 acres, more or less, and in one of the finest farms in Prince George's County. It lies along the line of the Baltimore and Potomac Railroad about one-quarter of a mile from Collington, where there will be a Depot on said road. The improvements are a large, two story brick dwelling house, 3 tobacco houses, corn house, granary, stables, servants' house, etc. The soil is well adapted to the growth of tobacco, corn, wheat, etc. Wood and water abundant.[11]

Responding to the auction notice in May 1871, Thomas Mumford and Henry A. Tayloe submitted a winning bid of $5,100 and gained ownership of the Belair property. Interestingly, George Ogle's prior stipulation had remained on the deed, and Rosalie Ogle was able to continue dwelling in the mansion. However, Rosalie allegedly took offense when the new owner's overseers moved in to the mansion, and she filed suit, alleging that she could not live with such "disagreeable people."[12] Rosalie vacated the property in 1871, effectively ending the Ogle era at Belair.

In 1877, Mumford and Tayloe sold Belair to Edward Rutter for the purchase price of $17,000. The property subsequently changed hands several times, parcels were divided and sometimes recombined and the once magnificent plantation and stud farm fell further into disarray. Finally, in 1898, Belair was purchased for an undisclosed sum by prominent New York banker James T. Woodward.

Chapter 4
THE EARLY WOODWARD ERA

At the time of its purchase in 1898, the Belair property displayed little of the splendor it had once known. The wood in many of the structures was rotted with age, and the mansion that had once entertained dignitaries was now a shadow of its former self. Trees that had formerly borne leaves and fruit were overridden with thorny weeds. The estate was in need of a complete overhaul, which would require serious planning and a significant amount of money.

If any man were strong enough to resurrect the Belair property, James Woodward was the premier candidate. An austere gentleman with gray hair and a stylish moustache, Woodward was gifted with both a keen business sense and the funds to back it up. He was extremely well respected in the business world, having brought New York's Hanover Bank to prosperity as its president. With Woodward at the helm, the bank's deposits increased from $6 million to $100 million. Woodward was also instrumental in the expansion of St. John's College in Annapolis and would later receive an honorary doctorate degree for his efforts.

James Woodward was born on September 27, 1837, at Edgewood Plantation in Gambrills Station, Maryland. His father, Henry, was a successful farmer who was descended from the Woodwards of colonial days, among the earliest settlers in the New World. During the years of the Civil War, James and his family generated substantial wealth by selling textiles to the Confederates. His older brother, William, had excelled in the family business and was a thriving textile merchant in New York City.

James Woodward's early studies took place in Maryland's local schools; he later moved to Baltimore to further his education. When the war ended, James relocated to New York, where he began working at an importing house called Ross, Campbell & Company and quickly made a name for himself. In the early 1870s, James became employed by the Hanover National Bank and rose to the position of director. Around 1877, James and his brother, William, partnered to purchase a large portion of the bank from its majority shareholders, merchants J&J Stewart. That same year, James was elected president of the bank, a position he would maintain for the remainder of his life.

Among his many professional accomplishments, James Woodward served as clearinghouse chairman during the financial panic of 1907. The *New York Times* later wrote of Woodward:

> *When the eyes of the financial world were focused on that body and bankers were fearful of what the next day might bring forth, his foresight, resourcefulness, and grasp on the situation came into national prominence. Before that, however, it had become well known, in New York at least, that the growth in the Hanover Bank in the last 25 years had been due largely to his ability.*[13]

The historic yet faltering Belair Stud held great interest for James Woodward, an accomplished horseman and gentleman farmer. Woodward enjoyed riding to hounds and was a member of several prominent equestrian and social clubs. After purchasing the estate, he would often travel to Belair on weekends so that he could enjoy the farm life and fox hunt on its lush acreage. According to the *New York Times*, Woodward "loved nothing better than to look over his livestock and prepare for the coming crops…and derived great pleasure from dilating to his friends about the beauties of Maryland and his life on the farm."[14]

James Woodward wasted no time in bringing Belair back to prosperity. He invested a significant amount of money in restoring the estate and purchased several adjacent tracts of land that had previously been sold off by the Ogles. Woodward hired a tree surgeon to restore the path of aged tulip poplars that lined Belair's lengthy drive. A new stable was constructed, the mansion was refurbished, crops were planted and animals such as horses, sheep and cattle were brought in. Woodward established several traditions, one of which was to raise the flag in the driveway when a member of the family was in residence at the farm.

Early view of the Belair Mansion. *Courtesy of the Belair Stable Museum.*

In 1900, Andrew Jackson, a former slave and jockey, was hired to care for the Thoroughbred horses and perform various other farm duties. Jackson, the son of former slaves, had become involved with racehorses as a boy in Kentucky. Jackson had subsequently traveled to New York, where he worked as a jockey for E.V. Snedeker, the trainer for Maryland governor Oden Bowie. Jackson piloted his mounts to wins in various races before retiring from riding in 1883. He subsequently became employed at Governor Bowie's farm, where he cared for the stable's colts for a period of nine years. Following the death of Governor Bowie, Jackson briefly worked as a store clerk before joining the staff at Belair.

Jackson would faithfully serve the Woodward family for the next thirty years and would play a pivotal role in the farm's early success. In addition to training and caring for the racehorses, Jackson managed the grade horses and ponies, drove carriages and performed many other duties at the estate. His affable nature was well received among both the Woodward family and the farm's various workers, who affectionately referred to him as "Uncle Andy."

Former jockey Andrew Jackson played a key role at Belair. *Courtesy of the Belair Stable Museum.*

Andrew Jackson was especially fond of James Woodward's nephew, William, a frequent visitor to the farm. The son of James's older brother, William Woodward was born in New York City on April 7, 1876. William's father, the founder of the New York Cotton Exchange, passed away when the boy was only thirteen years old. James took a special interest in his nephew, stepping into the role of a second father. He enrolled William at the prestigious Groton School, an esteemed preparatory institution in northern Massachusetts. William subsequently attended Harvard University, graduating magna cum laude before enrolling at Harvard Law in 1899. A talented athlete, William's activities at Groton and Harvard included varsity football and crew.

William Woodward was a highly intelligent young man who had great plans to revive Belair's Thoroughbred breeding and racing program. It was a seed that had been sown early on by his own father, who had taken the boy to races at nearby Jerome Park. William Woodward would later recall:

I think my love of Thoroughbred horses and racing came to me first about 1887, when I was 11 years old. In those days, my father used to take me every Decoration Day, May 30, to Jerome Park, which was about nine miles from our house in 51ˢᵗ Street, New York City. My father was very proud of his carriage horses and "turn out," as were all the well-known people of New York City at that time, and I can see him now sitting in the Duke with me at his side. The Duke was a large Victoria [carriage] swung on C springs, and occasionally a rumble was used in the rear for the groom, but in driving to Jerome Park, it being a considerable distance, the rumble was removed and two men sat in the box. We would arrive there in time for lunch and on the way out there would be numerous drags with their fine teams which would be going along with us. It made a gala sight and a pleasant holiday.

William Woodward, nephew of James Woodward. *Courtesy of the Belair Stable Museum.*

The first race that I really remember was the Belmont Stakes of 1888, in which Sir Dixon, the winner; and Prince Royal provided a stirring contest. I remember the colors and the whole scene. It was run in glorious sunshine.[15]

While still a young boy, William developed a lofty ambition for himself—to win the English Derby at Epsom. The Derby (pronounced "Dahr-bee") was founded in 1780 and was Britain's richest and most venerated race. In fact, the Kentucky Derby, the most prestigious event in American horse racing, was modeled after the Epsom Derby. William later recalled:

My father, who had always been interested in various sports, was at breakfast one morning with my mother, my sister, and myself, and I remember him saying Pierre Lorillard [with Iroquois, 1881] *is the first American to have won the English Derby. The remark made an impression on me, and I made up my mind (not knowing if I could ever own a race horse, or hardly what a race horse was) to be the second American to win the Derby.*[16]

William Woodward's goal to win the Epsom Derby would become a driving passion for the remainder of his lifetime. It was a passion that would propel him to excel in the world of racing and to bring his uncle's Belair Stud to the pinnacle of greatness.

Chapter 5

WILLIAM WOODWARD, MASTER OF BELAIR

B elair's William Woodward was the quintessential aristocrat—dashingly handsome, intelligent and dapper. He dressed impeccably, often donning a stylish top hat, wide-rimmed spectacles and an elegant moustache. In later years, he would carry a white-tipped cane, adding to his patrician flair. Tall and refined, Woodward spoke with an eloquent tone that was more befitting a British monarch than a New York banker.

William's immersion in British culture began after the completion of his studies at Harvard, when he was appointed as secretary to Joseph Choate, ambassador to the Court of St. James in England. There he befriended, among other luminaries, King Edward VII himself. The king, impressed with the young man's work ethic and passion for the sport, encouraged him to attend the races. Surrounded by royals at Ascot and Newmarket, William became thoroughly immersed in the ways of British racing. He learned the importance of impeccable breeding and patience in producing horses with the stamina to win distance races. According to *New York* magazine, this time in England allowed Woodward to "hone a lifelong practice of acting British" while nurturing his aspiration of one day winning the English Derby. In 1901, Woodward watched a second American accomplish this feat when New Yorker William C. Whitney's leased horse, Volodyovski, was victorious at Epsom. (Whitney was allegedly so thrilled with this triumph that he purchased champagne for everyone in attendance at Saratoga Race

Course that day.) Woodward later wrote: "Those were almost classic days in English racing, the days of Sceptre, Ard Patrick, William the Third, Rock Sand, Ballantrae, and many others—hence the basis for my love."[17]

With permission from the Marquis of Zetland in Yorkshire, William chose the colors, or silks, of his future racing stable. The Belair silks—oversized bright red dots on an ivory background—had been used by the Marquis as far back as the mid-1700s. The scarlet dotted silks would become a frequent sight at racetracks in both the United States and England in the coming years. The one difference between the Belair silks in the United States and England was the cap; Belair

The dapper William Woodward, master of Belair. *Courtesy of the Belair Stable Museum.*

jockeys in the United States donned red helmets, while the riders in England always wore black.

Upon completion of his two-year appointment in England, Woodward returned to the United States in 1903. While he had passed the bar and originally planned to practice law, Woodward joined his uncle James at the Hanover Bank and rose quickly into the position of director. Outside of the bank, William devoted himself to horse racing, bolstered by the knowledge he had gained in England. Together with his uncle James, William began his plans for breeding sturdy Thoroughbreds who could win the richest races in both the United States and abroad. He continued to study racing bloodlines and immersed himself in the intricacies of the sport. Weekends were spent on the racing circuit, which in the summer months turned to New York's Saratoga Race Course. Founded in 1863 by ex-boxer John Morrissey, the historic and picturesque racecourse was "the place to be" in August. It attracted not only the greatest horses but also the most elite members of New York society.

It was at Saratoga in the summer of 1903 that William Woodward met debutante Elizabeth "Elsie" Ogden Cryder. Outfitted in a pale yellow dress and daintily clutching a matching parasol, Elsie watched the races alongside her father. Elsie was a local celebrity of sorts, having achieved notoriety as one of the "Cryder triplets" born in 1882. Her father, Duncan, had been a prominent businessman and was one of the founders of Long Island's Shinnecock Hills Golf Club. In 1891, a banking scandal involving the girls' uncle had caused Duncan to flee with his family to Paris; there they lived what Elsie would describe as a "life of leisure" for the next several years. The family returned to New York in 1899, where the attractive and well-to-do triplets became the sensation of New York society. They were frequently followed by members of the media, who reported on the girls' attendance at various prominent social events. On one occasion, the triplets served as models for artist Charles Dana Gibson, creator of the famous "Gibson Girl" prototype.

Seated in a box at the Saratoga Race Course, the poised and stylish Elsie Cryder caught William Woodward's eye. She, in turn, was enamored with the aristocratic young man, and with the hearty blessings of Duncan Cryder, the two soon began courting. On October 24, 1904, William and Elsie were married at Grace Church in New York, in an event that the *New York Times* described as "a large and fashionable wedding." The couple's first child, named for Elsie's sister Edith, was born the next year; three more daughters, Elizabeth "Libby," Sarah and Ethel, would follow. The attractive and wealthy Woodwards became one of the area's most prominent couples, with Elsie later reigning as the "grand dame" of New York society.

While the Woodward family lived primarily in New York, William made regular visits to the Belair farm. On one such occasion, he learned that the estate of Governor Bowie was offering a band of mares for sale for $300. Bowie's Fairview Plantation in Maryland had once been a leading breeder of Thoroughbreds. The late Bowie had served as president of both the Maryland Jockey Club and the Pimlico Jockey Club and, in fact, was a founder of Pimlico Race Course and its most famous race, the Preakness Stakes.

The prospect of purchasing the group of mares was irresistible to William Woodward, who was interested in further expanding the Belair breeding stock. He later wrote:

> *I was at Belair with my uncle and found out about a bunch of Gov. Bowie's mares which had been in possession of his son, who had died. I bought three of them at $100 apiece. They were well-bred and in good condition, Bringing them to Belair, I needed some stalls for them and built three stalls at a cost of $100, for which my uncle made me pay—and he*

was quite right. The mares were all in foal, and I realized that by spring it would be necessary to have a stallion. Our old Negro, Andrew Jackson, who had been a jockey for Gov. Bowie, told me there was a stallion by the name of Capt. Hancock [Eolus—Belle d'Or, by Rayon d'Or] *that was standing as a country stallion, and he could be bought. I went to see him with some friends, and he looked like a bag of bones. But he had four legs and the necessary anatomy to serve my mares, and I bought him for $60. So, Belair Stud began with an expenditure of $360.*

I took Capt. Hancock to Belair and told Andrew that he had inveigled me into purchasing the horse and it was now up to him to get him into shape. He was exceedingly faithful in doing so, and two months later the horse looked like an Arab—sleek and beautiful.[18]

One of the mares from this purchase, the well-bred Charemma, would produce a filly in 1906 whom Woodward named Aile d'Or. According to racing historian and author Edward L. Bowen, the name was derived from "Fantasies, aux Aile d'Or," a song that Woodward had heard in a Parisian revue in 1900. Aile d'Or was trained by Andrew Jackson on the grounds of Belair, with Woodward riding alongside with his friend Phil "P.A." Clark. In due time, Aile d'Or earned a notable victory at Marlboro that effectively placed Belair on the racing map. Woodward later recalled: "We trained Aile d'Or on the country road, which was sandy at that time. I would ride a well-bred hunter, and a close friend of mine, P.A. Clark, would ride another, and we would station ourselves about 100 to 200 yards in front of the mare, she ridden by Andrew Jackson. This is the way we trained her, and she won. This can be called the first success of Belair Stud."[19]

Aile d'Or's role in the early success of Belair would become apparent in the coming years. In 1916, she produced Lion d'Or, Belair Stud's first stakes winner. A son of Heno, Lion d'Or's wins would include the 1920 Toboggan Handicap, Fall HighWeight Cap, Baldwin HighWeight Cap and Queens Co. Cap., recorded under the ownership of P.A. Clark. It is interesting to note that Woodward occasionally entered horses in the early years under Clark's name rather than his own. According to some sources, Woodward's motive was to conceal his racing endeavors from the possible disapproval of Hanover Bank colleagues.

On April 10, 1910, James Woodward passed away after a brief illness, leaving William as the official master of Belair. Flags were flown at half-mast in James's honor on Wall Street, as well as at the various clubs to which he had belonged. James had died a bachelor, and his entire estate (which also included the Cloisters mansion in Newport, Rhode Island) was bequeathed to his nephew. According to historian Shirley Baltz, the inheritance tax totaled $3,200, which was the highest amount ever paid in Prince Georges County at that time. William also succeeded his uncle as president of the Hanover Bank.

As he began his tenure as master of Belair, William purchased several adjacent tracts of land, further increasing the farm's vast acreage. He continued to renovate the mansion and stables and expanded the breeding program with the addition of several prized broodmares. In 1914, Woodward and P.A. Clark were visiting Newport when they heard of the sale of some mares sired by the French stallion Ajax. A son of the great Flying Fox, Ajax's wins had included the Prix du Jockey Club, Grand Prix de Paris, Prix de St. Fermin, Prix Lupin and Prix Noailles. Woodward wrote:

In 1914, I had a bit of good fortune. It was during the days of World War I when the Germans were marching on Paris, and I was exceedingly busy in New York with no time to spare and rarely went up to Newport, where my family was spending the summer. But one Sunday I was there for 24 hours and Phil Clark and I were reading newspapers under the trees that morning. I saw a short paragraph in the New York Times *that M. Edmond Blanc, who then owned the greatest stud in France, was selling a number of his horses at Cheri's sales in Paris on Monday, the following day, and they were listed. I said to Clark that there were five by Ajax that I would love to buy. He said, "Why not buy them?" I said, "It seems quite impossible as they're to be sold in about 20 hours from now, in Paris."*

He suggested that he ask George Blumenthal of Lazard Freres to cable his partner, Michael Lazard, who was a French racing man, to buy them for me.[20]

The plan developed by Woodward and Clark proved to be successful. Woodward conveyed his interest in the purchase, with two stipulations. No individual horse would be purchased for more than $3,750, and the total purchase of the five animals would not exceed $7,500. To Woodward's benefit, the entire band was ultimately purchased for $3,750. There was one problem, however. The French authorities, in an effort to preserve the Thoroughbred bloodlines, had enacted restrictions for exporting Thoroughbreds. Only the yearling was allowed to be shipped to the United States, and sadly, she died during the rough overseas journey.

The four remaining mares were housed at the farm of Frenchman Jules Jariel until the export restrictions were lifted. Grain was scarce during these wartime years, and as a result, the mares grew painfully thin. When the herd finally arrived at Belair years later, Woodward was distraught at the sight of their condition.

Ever the patient horseman, Woodward developed a careful plan for bringing the mares back to health. Breeding was postponed, and the mares were lightly exercised as they regained their strength on the lush Belair pastures. Woodward's care and patience paid off, and the prized animals were returned to good health. As an added plus, the broodmare La Flambee had produced two fillies for Woodward while still in France: the two-year-old La Rablee (by the leading French sire Rabelais) and the yearling Flambette (by French Derby Stakes winner Durbar II).

The Ajax mares and fillies would become valuable additions to Belair Stud in the years to come. Flambette would win two key races in 1918: the Coaching Club American Oaks at Belmont Park and the Latonia Oaks in Kentucky. After retirement, she would become an important member of the Belair broodmare band; her offspring would include the filly Flambino, who would in turn become the dam of one of Belair's greatest champions.

Flambette's victory in the Coaching Club American Oaks was a source of enormous pride for Woodward, who, as a member of the Coaching Club of America, was one of the founders of the race. One of the requirements for membership in the club was the ability to handle a coach and four horses with a single group of reins. In October 1916, Woodward and several fellow members of the club (including August Belmont Jr., breeder of Man o' War) left New York on a coaching trip to Belair Stud. The journey was covered by the *New York Times*, whose report on October 11 included the following:

> *The start was made from the Knickerbocker Club early this morning… forty horses were collected for the drive, the Knickerbocker stable supplying five teams. The horses used on the first day will be sent forward by rail in express cars to be drawn again on the third day, and those used on the second day will be forwarded in the same way for the fourth.*
>
> *The travelers took their turns at driving, Mr. William Woodward taking the horses across Statten [sic] Island. August Belmont drove the team as far as Metuchen.*[21]

One of the members, F.K. Sturgis, reported: "That portion of the trip which impressed us all…was the final stage, on which Mr. Woodward furnished the horses. There were four Thoroughbreds, while the cockhorse

Above: William Woodward's coaching trip to Belair, 1916. *Courtesy of the Belair Stable Museum.*

Below: The Belair Mansion in 1916. *Courtesy of the Belair Stable Museum.*

The coaching club arrives at Belair. *Courtesy of the Belair Stable Museum.*

was also clean berd, and there wasn't one of them under 16 hands…We remained at Bellair [*sic*] House until 3:30 PM on Sunday, and returned to New York by train."[22]

In addition to the Coaching Club of America, William Woodward was a respected member of various other important organizations. In 1917, he was elected to the United States Jockey Club and would serve as its chairman from 1930 until 1950. Additionally, in recognition of his efforts overseas, he would be elected an honorary member of the British Jockey Club.

William Woodward was a methodical planner, and the turn of the decade into the 1920s served as a platform for the further development of Belair Stud. It was also a time of great happiness for Woodward on a personal level, as his only son, William Jr. (known as Billy), was born on June 12, 1920. As he notified his friends in the racing industry, Woodward's words beamed with the pride of a true horseman. The cable announcing Billy's birth simply read, "Fine colt born this morning."

Chapter 6

THE ROARING TWENTIES

As the United States experienced prosperity in the early 1920s, William Woodward worked tirelessly to develop his Belair Stud farm. Structural improvements at this time included a complete renovation of the stable; as preventive measures, wood was replaced with brick and several doors were added for easy access to the horses in case of fire. The stables now included north and south sections, with the stalls brightly painted in the red-and-white stable colors of Belair Stud. The North Stable housed the carriage and riding horses, which included fox hunters and ponies for the children, while the South Stable served as a dwelling for the racehorses. Woodward also hired an on-site stable manager and converted one of the carriage houses to a caretaker's residence.

Woodward also continued to expand his band of breeding stock at this time. At Saratoga's yearling consignment sale in 1921, Woodward purchased a yearling filly by the name of Marguerite. The filly had been bred by Arthur B. Hancock, master of Claiborne Farm in Paris, Kentucky. Hancock had been virtually born into the horse industry, as his father, Captain Richard Johnson Hancock, was a noted Thoroughbred breeder at his Ellerslie Stud in Virginia. Arthur had continued the family tradition, combining Ellerslie with a farm in Kentucky that belonged to his wife's family. The resulting Claiborne Farm would become one of the greatest breeding operations in history, standing the most illustrious Thoroughbred stallions. In the years to follow, Woodward and Hancock would develop a successful partnership in which the Belair mares would

Stable worker Ben Brady with a Belair horse in 1920. *Courtesy of the Belair Stable Museum.*

be bred and drop their foals at Claiborne and the colts and fillies would return to Belair after weaning.

The chestnut filly Marguerite was a daughter of Celt, the leading American sire of 1921. Upon arriving at Belair, the filly was prepared for a career in racing, but fate interrupted with an alternate plan. In her first and only start, Marguerite sustained a back injury that forced her into early retirement. She would prove invaluable as a broodmare, however, as evidenced by her first mating to the English stallion Wrack. The resulting colt, Petee-Wrack, would become a major stakes winner whose victories included the 1928 Suburban, Metropolitan and Travers Stakes. Sold by Woodward as a yearling, Petee-Wrack raced under the colors of John R. Macomber.

In addition to its Thoroughbred horses, Belair continued to house a wide array of farm animals, including cattle, fowl, pigs and sheep. In 1918, Belair made national headlines when Woodward lent twelve Shropshire sheep and four lambs to President Woodrow Wilson to graze the White House lawn to reduce wartime landscaping expenses. The sheep were well received by

White House staff and the media, who photographed the animals grazing happily on the lawn at 1600 Pennsylvania Avenue. When the sheep were shorn in May of that same year, the resulting wool was auctioned off, generating nearly $50,000 for charities such as the American Red Cross and the War Fund. The sheep were returned to Belair in 1920, along with a note of thanks from the president and Mrs. Wilson. William Woodward responded with a note that concluded, "The memory of [their] stay on the White House grounds will always be treasured at Belair."[23]

As Belair continued to operate as a full working farm, workhorses were also kept on the property. Woodward was a noted breeder of Clydesdale horses, which were used for farm chores such as plowing the corn and wheat fields. In later years, the well-bred Clydesdales would be nationally renowned, garnering various trophies at fairs and other competitions. The horses were exhibited at the Maryland State Fair and appeared at various other events, including the Cherry Blossom Parade. According to the Belair Stable Museum, both the Ringling Bros. Circus and the Anheuser-Busch Company purchased Clydesdale horses from Belair.

Belair sheep on the White House lawn. *Courtesy of the Belair Stable Museum.*

The prized Belair Clydesdales. *Courtesy of the Belair Stable Museum.*

The year 1923 served as a turning point at Belair, as Woodward hired James Fitzsimmons to train the stable's Thoroughbreds. Affectionately known as "Sunny Jim" for his cheerful Irish countenance, the trainer was born in 1874 in the Sheepshead Bay section of Brooklyn. He began work as a dishwasher in the track kitchen at a young age, progressing to the role of stable boy at the age of eleven. Fitzsimmons subsequently worked as a jockey for several years, riding his first winner in 1890. However, he had little success as a rider and, struggling with weight issues, opted to switch to training. In 1900, Fitzsimmons saddled his first winner, Agnes D., at Brighton Beach for owner Colonel Edward Morell. With several other winners credited to his name, "Mr. Fitz" was hired by Woodward as the trainer for Belair Stud.

Woodward and Fitzsimmons shared a genuine respect for each other; in fact, despite working together for the next thirty years, the two men never signed a formal agreement. Rather, the deals were forged with handshakes, a gentlemen's agreement between owner and trainer. The partnership of Woodward with Jim Fitzsimmons would prove monumental in the later success of Belair Stud.

With Mr. Fitz secured as Belair's trainer, Woodward continued to focus on the breeding program. In 1925, he joined Hancock and fellow breeders Robert A. Fairburn and Marshall Field III in a syndicate to import the

Belair's trainer, Sunny Jim Fitzsimmons. *Courtesy of the Belair Stable Museum.*

French stallion Sir Gallahad III. The horse, sired by the fashionable Teddy out of the mare Plucky Liege, was a talented runner, having won twelve races in Europe for his British breeder/owner, Jefferson Davis Cohn. As a two-year-old, Sir Gallahad was victorious in three of his five starts but was eclipsed by Pierre Wertheimer's precocious colt, Epinard, for year-end

Above: Sunny Jim Fitzsimmons and William Woodward. *Courtesy of the Belair Stable Museum.*

Right: Elsie and William Woodward (seated) with Sunny Jim Fitzsimmons. *Courtesy of the Belair Stable Museum.*

honors. Returning to the track at the age of three, Sir Gallahad won four races (including the French 2,000 Guineas), despite raising eyebrows when he dumped his rider and dove into a nearby pond at the Grand Prix de Paris. The following year brought with it stellar success for Sir Gallahad, as the colt topped three key races in France, as well as England's Lincolnshire Handicap. That season, he also bested his rival, Epinard, in a highly touted match race over six and a half furlongs.

In December 1925, Sir Gallahad III was loaded onto the luxury steamship *Minnetonka II* in London to begin his journey to the United States. Purchased by the syndicate for $125,000, the stallion stood at Hancock's Claiborne Farm, where he was mated with Woodward's mare Marguerite in 1926.

The decision to import Sir Gallahad would prove to be a colossal judgment for the future of American horse racing. The horse would eventually top the U.S. general sire list four times and the broodmare sire list twelve times. He would produce sixty-five stakes winners, including three Kentucky Derby champions, and his daughters would beget future Hall of Famers Challedon and Gallorette. According to historian Anne Peters:

Sir Gallahad III, sire of Gallant Fox. *Courtesy of the Library of Congress.*

Sir Gallahad was a landmark in more than one regard. Not only was he purchased by the first modern stallion "syndicate," but he became the sire that put Arthur Hancock's Claiborne Farm on the map as a home to world class stallions. And although it was not known at the time, his sire and dam were to prove a pair of the most influential thoroughbreds of the century, and Sir Gallahad himself, one of the most important sires, and sire of broodmares in America.[24]

Chapter 7

THE FOX OF BELAIR

On March 23, 1927, the mating of Sir Gallahad with the mare Marguerite produced a leggy bay colt. The new foal, named Gallant Fox, was gallant indeed, with an attractive wide blaze and splashes of ivory above all four hooves. He also had a "wall eye," a condition in which the iris lacks pigment and is surrounded by a light ring. According to some sources, William Woodward believed that Gallant Fox's optical defect would provide a distinct advantage on the racetrack, as other horses would be frightened and unwilling to pass the colt with the "evil eye."

Gallant Fox followed the typical schedule of Woodward's Belair program. He was foaled at Arthur Hancock's Claiborne Farm in Kentucky and shipped to Belair as a weanling. Each spring, Woodward and Mr. Fitz would drive along the rows of paddocks in the farm's Ford truck, inspecting each yearling for a spark of impending greatness. Together, the experienced trainer and owner would decide which yearlings they would keep and which would be sold at Saratoga. Additionally, four horses would be designated to be shipped to England, where they would school under Belair's overseas trainer, the famed Cecil Boyd-Rochfort, at his Freemason Lodge at Newmarket. Woodward had a solid partnership with Boyd-Rochfort, who for many years would prepare Belair's UK string for the English classic races. Those horses who remained in the United States would be broken to saddle and then sent on to Fitzsimmons's home track of Aqueduct for training.

The striking bay Gallant Fox fit into the latter category. After completing his early schooling, he was shipped to New York for training under the keen

Above: The handsome Gallant Fox. *Courtesy of the Belair Stable Museum.*

Below: Sunny Jim Fitzsimmons inspects an unnamed yearling (held by stable employee Charles Thomas). *Courtesy of the Belair Stable Museum.*

eye of Jim Fitzsimmons. Gallant Fox was unique from his earliest days as a youngster. Unlike many young colts, who can be quite fractious, Gallant Fox possessed a pleasant temperament and enjoyed the company of humans. He also was lazy and curious, however—traits that are not particularly desirable in a champion racehorse. Author Jimmy Breslin, in his biography of Mr. Fitz, wrote of the horse:

> *Gallant Fox was, in Fitzsimmons' barn in Aqueduct, about as lazy an animal as anybody ever came across. He would run with another horse in the morning, then stop dead the minute he passed him…In his first couple of starts, Gallant Fox was well out of it. But Mr. Fitz saw one thing in him: the horse was coming on at the end every time…it looked like he simply needed more ground to cover.*[25]

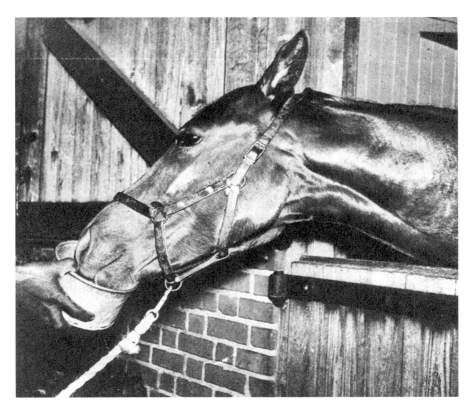

Gallant Fox is fed in his stall. *Courtesy of the Belair Stable Museum.*

Gallant Fox made his racing debut at Aqueduct on June 24, 1929, with less than stellar results. In a five-furlong allowance race, the colt placed a disappointing third. Under Belair's rigorous racing schedule, his next start would come less than one week later. Mr. Fitz was known for racing his horses at frequent intervals, believing that it built up a horse's stamina. It was a strategy that would prove to be successful; however, Gallant Fox would take a while to adjust to the program. In his second start, in Belmont's Tremont Stakes, Gallant Fox placed a frustrating eighth. However, the reason for the loss had nothing to do with the colt's talent. As the race began, Gallant Fox was so preoccupied by the sounds of an airplane flying overhead that he failed to break with the other starters and fell miserably behind.

The Tremont was to be Gallant Fox's only career finish out of the money. He broke his maiden in his next start on July 29 at Saratoga, besting William R. Coe's Caruso by one and a half lengths. Continuing on Mr. Fitz's schedule, the two colts met again four days later for Saratoga's U.S. Hotel Stakes. This time, Caruso got the best of Gallant Fox, with the two colts carrying equal weight. In his next start in the Futurity Trial at Belmont, the Fox overcame traffic, gaining steadily and placing himself within a neck of the winner, the gray colt Polygamous. The Futurity was next, and Gallant Fox placed third behind the eventual juvenile champion, Harry Payne Whitney's colt Whichone, winner of the Champagne and Saratoga Special Stakes races. Gallant Fox's final start as a juvenile was the Junior Champion Stakes at Aqueduct, and the colt made the race his own. He defeated the eventual Kentucky Jockey Club Stakes winner Desert Light by two lengths, despite carrying five additional pounds.

While Gallant Fox failed to win two-year-old championship honors, the colt had gained valuable experience in his maiden season. By all accounts, William Woodward was never focused on juvenile honors and had his sights firmly set on the classic races. Under the structured program of the wise Mr. Fitz, Gallant Fox matured over the following months. His bay coat gleamed, he cleaned up his feed and mentally he seemed well prepared for the spring racing season.

As the first races of 1930 loomed large in the foreground, William Woodward was poised to make one final adjustment. Having been ridden by several jockeys as a two-year-old, Gallant Fox never had the benefit of a regular rider. Woodward, a true horseman, was highly aware that the ongoing partnership between a horse and rider can be a strong component in a winning strategy. Woodward brought the matter to Mr. Fitz's attention, and the two men agreed to discuss likely candidates. According to author

Richard J. Maturi in *The Earl Sande Saga*, Woodward and Fitz agreed to develop a short list of potential jockeys who could possibly be hired to ride Gallant Fox. When they compared lists, Woodward and Fitz found that they had scribbled the names of the same two riders.

The first potential jockey for Gallant Fox was the talented and experienced Clarence Kummer. Thirty-one-year-old Kummer had a long list of accomplishments. In 1919, he had set a track record on the great Sir Barton in winning the Saratoga Handicap. The following year, he had ridden the immortal Man o' War to nine straight victories after the retirement of regular jockey Johnny Loftus. Kummer had more recently struggled to maintain weight and was forced into retirement after the 1928 season. By 1930, however, Kummer was working toward a possible return to racing.

The other potential match for Gallant Fox was jockey Earl Sande. Along with Kummer, Sande was one of the top jockeys of the 1920s. He had been the leading money winner in the United States in both 1921 and 1923, an achievement he duplicated in 1927. Sande's mounts had included Zev, winner of both the Kentucky Derby and the Belmont Stakes in 1923. That same year, the jockey's fame rose to new heights when he and Zev defeated Epsom Derby winner Papyrus by five lengths in a thrilling match race. Similar to Kummer, however, Sande had retired from riding, plagued by various injuries, weight issues and the recent death of his wife. It was rumored that Sande was planning a comeback, having lost a substantial amount of money in the stock market crash.

When William Woodward heard that Sande had already renewed his license, the master of Belair sent a telegraph to the jockey. Sande responded, proposing that the two meet at New York's Jamaica racetrack the following week. At the close of the meeting, Woodward offered Sande a contract for the season. The jockey, however, declined Woodward's offer, suggesting instead that the two men sign an introductory one-race deal. Under this contract, Sande could prove to Woodward that his riding was up to par, while the jockey could gain a genuine feel for the Belair colt. Woodward agreed, and the two men sealed the deal with a firm handshake.

The one race under this agreement was Gallant Fox's three-year-old debut in the Wood Memorial at Jamaica. The race, a key prep for the Kentucky Derby, marked Sande's return to racing in well over a year. As the media speculated as to whether the new pairing would be successful, Sande and the Fox quieted any possible doubts. Closing strong after being boxed in for much of the race, the pair defeated Youthful Stakes winner Crack Brigade by four lengths for the win. The *New York Times* heralded "The Fox of Belair" as a favorite for the spring classics, noting, "The Belair Stud's Gallant Fox, with Earl Sande riding his first New York race since September, 1928, came home first in a gallop in the Wood Memorial at Jamaica yesterday, creating more enthusiasm as to his prospects in the Preakness and Kentucky Derby than has been shown about a horse in years."[26]

Following the Wood Memorial victory, Woodward offered Sande a generous payment of $10,000 for the season, in addition to regular riding fees. While many riders would have leapt at such an offer, Sande once again had his own negotiations, proposing instead a compensation of 10 percent of any purse monies won. Once again, Woodward agreed, and Sande became Gallant Fox's regular jockey.

Amid great fanfare, Sande and Gallant Fox took to the track at Pimlico on May 9 for the Preakness Stakes, which at that time was held prior to the Kentucky Derby. While Sande had been victorious in numerous key races, the Preakness Stakes had somehow continuously eluded him. The media speculated as to whether the "Preakness Curse" would continue to plague the jockey or if the great Fox of Belair would be the one to break the spell. The betting fans believed in Gallant Fox, who entered the race as the 9–5 favorite. Fans cheered wildly as the handsome bay completed the post parade, donning the cheerful Belair silks. The nation was in the throes of the Great Depression, and Americans were desperately in search of a hero. Drawn by the Fox's appearance and the popularity of Earl Sande, more than forty thousand spectators lined the stands at Pimlico Race Course.

The 1930 Preakness would be unusual in more than one way. The race marked the introduction of a stall machine, a precursor to the starting gates of today. In the early years, races had been started by a drum tap, which coincided with the dropping of a flag. Horses were called to the track area by a bell, and a string was stretched across the track to call the horses into position. Later, a web barrier was used. As these methods were not without their problems, the starting gate was meant to simplify the process.

Gallant Fox handled the stall machine like a champ. He broke smoothly from the inside position before being passed by his old foe Crack Brigade and the British-bred Tetrarchal. At the first turn, the Fox ran into trouble, boxed inside the pack and lagging six lengths behind the leaders. Approaching the backstretch, Sande urged the Fox to the outside, his eyes firmly focused on the eight horses in their path. Opening up his stride, the Fox ultimately reached the leaders, surging past Tetrarchal before galloping neck-and-neck with Crack Brigade. As the two champions battled for position, the roars of the crowd propelled the Fox farther forward, and he bested Crack

Gallant Fox and Earl Sande at the Preakness. *Courtesy of the Belair Stable Museum.*

Brigade by three-quarters of a length. Not only had Sande's Preakness Curse been broken, but his financial worries were about to decrease as well. Under the terms of his proposed agreement, the jockey earned more than $5,000—more than half of the total salary he would have earned under William Woodward's original offer.

From Pimlico it was on to Churchill Downs for the Kentucky Derby, the second of the three spring classic races. Days of pelting rain had rendered the dirt track at Churchill Downs sloppy, but the Fox of Belair would handle it in stride. Breaking well from the gate, Gallant Fox was boxed in close quarters for the first three-eighths of a mile before taking the lead. The *Daily Racing Form* reported that Gallant Fox "raced into the lead on the outside after straightening out in the backstretch, held command under restraint thereafter and won with something in reserve."

After the race, a smiling Sande remarked, "Gallant Fox is a great horse, one of the best I ever rode…Gallant Fox won this [Kentucky] Derby by himself and never gave me a moment's worry…It was the easiest of the three Derbies I won."[27] Gallant Fox's victory catapulted Sande's name into horse-racing history, as he had also captured the Run for the Roses aboard Zev in 1923 and Flying Ebony in 1925. Only one other jockey, the great Isaac Murphy, had won three Kentucky Derbys at that time.

In attendance for the Fox's win, and seated alongside William Woodward, was Edward George Villiers Stanley, seventeenth earl of Derby. As Gallant Fox crossed the wire, Lord Derby turned to Mr. Woodward and deemed the victory "fine stuff."

Gallant Fox (Earl Sande, up) is led by William Woodward at Belmont. *Courtesy of the Belair Stable Museum.*

Following the Derby win, Gallant Fox headed to Belmont, where he would face a new set of challenges. The champion colt Whichone, who had been sidelined with an injury that had kept him out of both the Preakness and the Derby, was back in great form. Whichone, appearing sleek and ready for battle, had just come off a four-length victory in the Withers Stakes at Aqueduct and was, in fact, sent off as the top betting choice. Another challenge would be posed by Earl Sande's physical state. Two nights prior to the Belmont, Sande was a passenger in an automobile accident and sustained several injuries to his face and hands.

Sande had overcome numerous obstacles in his life and was not about to give up easily. He gave the race his best effort, leading Gallant Fox and the Belair silks to a wire-to-wire victory over Whichone for the mile and a half. Questionnaire, a multiple stakes winner, placed third. With this victory, Gallant Fox became the all-time money winner to date and the second U.S. Triple Crown champion. Interestingly, while another colt, Sir Barton, had won the trio of races in 1919, it was Gallant Fox's capture of the three that first led to the coinage of the phrase "Triple Crown." Charles Hatton of the *Daily Racing Form* is typically credited with the first reference in describing Gallant Fox's sweep of the three races. Around that same time, Bryan Field, a columnist for the *New York Times*, wrote, "Earl Sande gave all the credit to his mount which by winning the Preakness, Kentucky Derby, and Belmont had equaled the feat of Sir Barton. These two horses are the only ones to win the 'triple crown.'"[28]

After handing Belair Stud its first Triple Crown, Gallant Fox continued his winning ways, capturing the Dwyer Stakes at Belmont and besting Derby runner-up Gallant Knight by a neck in Chicago's Arlington Classic. By that time, Gallant Fox had been lauded as one of the sport's all-time greats, with the *Boston Globe* referring to him as "America's greatest race horse since Man o' War."

Heading to Saratoga for the summer classics, Gallant Fox received a welcome befitting his heroic status. On the day of the Travers Stakes, Saratoga's "mid-summer Derby," cars lined up for nearly two miles past the racecourse's main gates. The Travers attracted a record crowd, which included Franklin Delano Roosevelt, then serving as governor of New York. The race was touted as a showdown between Gallant Fox and Whichone, and the two colts were poised for a thrilling duel. Whichone was armed to avenge his Belmont defeat, having recently added the Saranac Stakes to his illustrious list of wins.

Sunny Jim feeds Gallant Fox at Saratoga. *Courtesy of the Belair Stable Museum.*

Saratoga's famed track is well known for its thunderstorms, and Travers Day 1930 was no exception. A summer deluge had muddied the track, rendering it a continuous puddle of slop. Gallant Fox was sent off as the betting favorite at odds of 1–2, with Whichone following closely behind. Just as anticipated, as the gates opened, Earl Sande on the Fox and Sonny Workman on Whichone immediately entered into a thrilling high-tempo duel. While the two battled down the stretch, a 100–1 long shot named Jim Dandy made his move, passing the two champions and ultimately winning the race by eight lengths over the tiring Gallant Fox. Whichone broke down in the stretch, suffering a career-ending injury. The race would become known as perhaps the biggest upset in the history of the Travers Stakes, with Saratoga cementing its reputation as the "graveyard of favorites." (In homage to this upset, in 1964, Saratoga established the Jim Dandy Stakes, which has since become a key prep race for the modern-day Travers.)

Gallant Fox avenged the loss to Jim Dandy with a win over older horses in the fourteen-furlong Saratoga Cup and a subsequent defeat of Questionnaire at $1^5/_8$ miles in the Lawrence Realization Stakes. The Fox completed his classic season with a victory in the Jockey Club Gold Cup at two miles, solidifying his position as both champion three-year-old colt and horse of the year. By the time of his retirement at year's end, Gallant Fox had amassed eleven wins and five seconds in seventeen starts, with winnings of $328,165. His 1930 season earnings of $308,275 set a new record in the sport.

With continued comparisons to Man o' War and other immortals, Gallant Fox's accomplishments had placed him in elite company. In September

Gallant Fox wins the Lawrence Realization Stakes. *Courtesy of the Belair Stable Museum.*

Gallant Fox at Claiborne Farm. *Courtesy of the Belair Stable Museum.*

1930, Colonel Walter Moriarty of the *National Turf Digest* wrote: "Few horses in any country have really earned the right to be called 'great'…Gallant Fox is a great horse. If he never wins another race, he will go down in history as one of the best ever bred in any country."[29]

Following his retirement, Gallant Fox was sent to Claiborne Farm to begin his next phase of life as a breeding stallion. He would live a long and prosperous life at Claiborne, siring twenty-two stakes winners before his death at the age of twenty-seven. Gallant Fox remained one of the favorite horses of his owner, who penned and published a biography of the horse entitled *Gallant Fox: A Memoir* in 1931. Additionally, Woodward hired sculptress Eleanor Iselin to create a bronze likeness of the horse. According to sources, Woodward was so fond of the sculpture that he carried it with him on numerous occasions. Beginning with Gallant Fox, Woodward also began a lasting tradition in which an artist was commissioned to paint a portrait of Belair's best horse each season; similarly, the annual Belair Christmas card featured a likeness of that year's greatest champion.

In honor of Gallant Fox, a handicap race bearing his name was instituted in 1939 at New York's Jamaica racetrack. In a fitting bow to the great Fox of Belair, the inaugural winner, Isolater, was a Belair Stud horse.

Chapter 8

OMAHA, THE BELAIR BULLET

Retired to stud at Arthur Hancock's Claiborne Farm, Gallant Fox sired a leggy chestnut colt out of the mare Flambino in his first foal crop. Flambino, a daughter of the British champion Wrack, won the Gazelle Stakes and placed third in the 1927 Belmont Stakes.

The new colt was as flashy as his sire, with splashes of white on both hind legs and a handsome wide blaze. He was given the name of Omaha, as William Woodward had traced his lineage back to the stallion Ormonde (winner of the Epsom Derby) and desired a name that also began with the letter O. According to sources, Omaha was the first name that came to Woodward's mind. Contrary to popular belief, the colt was not named for the city of Omaha, Nebraska.

Omaha began his racing career with a disappointing loss on June 18, 1934, beaten by a mere nose in a maiden race. Five days later, the long-limbed colt was in winning form, breaking his maiden in a five-furlong allowance race at Aqueduct. While hopes were high for the son of Gallant Fox, Omaha was yet to win again as a two-year-old. After finishing fourth in both the U.S. Hotel Stakes and the Saratoga Special, Omaha showed promise in the Sanford Memorial, placing second behind the eventual winner, Psychic Bid. The two met again in Saratoga's Hopeful Stakes for juveniles, but Omaha was unable to catch the leaders and ultimately finished fourth. He once again showed promise in the Champagne Stakes, losing in a photo finish as the winner, the eventual juvenile champion Balladier, galloped away with a new track record. Omaha finished out of the money in the Futurity before rebounding

Triple Crown winner Omaha. *Courtesy of the Belair Stable Museum.*

once more in another close second-place finish, this time in the Junior Champion Stakes. By season's end, Omaha had amassed only one win and had finished out of the money in four of his nine starts.

Over the winter, Omaha began to fill out and suddenly took on the appearance of a champion. At close to seventeen hands, he was larger than his sire. According to sources, Omaha's size often required a double stall in order for the horse to be comfortable. To accomplish this, many racetracks were forced to remove the partition between two existing stalls to accommodate the large colt.

Omaha began his classic season with a win in an overnight allowance race at Aqueduct and then finished a game third behind Today and Plat Eye in the Wood Memorial. Omaha was ridden in these races by Canadian jockey Willie "Smokey" Saunders. The jockey was the choice of Fitzsimmons, who had been impressed by Saunders's win on Belair's Faireno in the Rochambeau Handicap the prior season.

After Omaha's solid finish in the Wood, the colt headed to the Triple Crown races that had been won by his sire five years earlier. By this time, the Kentucky Derby at Churchill Downs was the first of the three races in the series. Omaha was sent off as the second betting choice in the Derby, with Calumet Farm's Nellie Flag deemed the odds-on favorite. The filly was piloted by nineteen-year-old jockey Eddie Arcaro, who was riding in his first-ever Run for the Roses.

Despite the public's high hopes for Nellie Flag, the filly was to finish out of the money. Soaring across the hallowed dirt at Churchill Downs, Omaha galloped from the outside post to gain the lead, winning by one and a half lengths over Roman Soldier and Whiskolo. According to the *Daily Racing Form*'s race recap, "Omaha escaped interference in the early crowding, was taken to the outside after the first quarter, raced to the lead gradually after reaching the half-mile post and held sway thereafter, winning easily."

Following Omaha's Derby win, the media swarmed around William Woodward, questioning the master of Belair for his predictions on the coming races. The media was particularly interested in knowing if Woodward believed that Omaha would follow in the hoof prints of Gallant Fox and bring another Triple Crown home to Belair. The eloquent Woodward simply responded that he hoped Omaha "would be just like" his sire.

In the Preakness Stakes the following week, Omaha showed that comparisons to his sire were warranted, winning by six lengths over Mr. and Mrs. Walter Jeffords's colt, Firethorn, and Hopeful Stakes champion Psychic Bid. However, a loss in the Withers Stakes at Aqueduct gave fodder to

Omaha is led by owner William Woodward. *Courtesy of the Belair Stable Museum.*

some of Omaha's critics, who felt that the colt was not equipped to handle the distance of the Belmont Stakes.

Four contenders took to a rain-soaked track at Belmont to try to prevent Omaha from winning the Triple Crown. Among them was the popular Rosemont, who had defeated Omaha in the Withers (and would subsequently defeat Seabiscuit in the Santa Anita Handicap). As the gate opened, the early lead went to Alfred G. Vanderbilt's Cold Shoulder, who was passed in approaching the stretch run by a driving Firethorn. In a thrilling finish, Omaha passed the brown Sun Briar colt, winning the race by one and a half lengths and duplicating his sire's great feat in winning the Triple Crown for Belair. The *Blood Horse* wrote:

> *Amid hearty cheering, Saunders brought Omaha back to the winner's circle, the victory being the most popular of the day. There, despite a driving rain, waited Omaha's owner, William Woodward, and the New York banker led in, for the second time in his Turf career, a horse which had won the Kentucky Derby, Preakness and Belmont Stakes in his colors. The first, in 1930, was Gallant Fox, sire of the present 3-year-old champion, now indisputably at the top of his division.*[30]

Omaha at the Belmont Stakes with jockey Willie Saunders. *Courtesy of the Belair Stable Museum.*

Omaha's thrilling Triple Crown sweep was followed by a disappointing third-place finish against older horses in the Brooklyn Handicap, a race that was won by the colt Discovery, known as the "Iron Horse" for his ability to carry high weights. Omaha returned to winning form with a blazing victory in the mile-and-an-eighth Dwyer Stakes on June 29, finishing the race in 1:49 $^1/_5$ and equaling the time set by the immortal Man o' War. In his final race of the season, Omaha defeated the champion filly Black Helen in the Arlington Classic, setting a new track record for a three-year-old at a mile and a quarter in 2:01 $^2/_5$.

Omaha's blistering bursts of speed impressed race-goers and media alike, who nicknamed the striking chestnut the "Belair Bullet." The season ended with frustration, however, when Omaha was injured during a pre-Travers workout at Saratoga and was forced to retire for the remainder of the season. In a further disappointment for Woodward and Belair, the colt Discovery—and not Omaha—was named Horse of the Year at season's end. The "Iron Horse," carrying weights of up to 139 pounds, had won eleven of nineteen starts that season. (To date, this would be the only instance in which a Triple Crown winner would fail to be named Horse of the Year.)

As Omaha recovered over the next several months, Woodward opted to send the champion to train with Cecil Boyd-Rochfort in England. Crowds cheered wildly as the four-year-old Omaha boarded the RMS *Aquitania* in January 1936 and was sent off to prepare for the Ascot Gold Cup. The Belair Bullet made his first UK start in the mile-and-a-half Victor Wild Stakes on May 9, winning handily by a solid length and a half. The colt then impressed the British public when he won the Queen's Plate over two miles at Kempton Park Racecourse, carrying the high weight of 130 pounds.

Nearly 200,000 spectators were on hand at Ascot on June 18 as Omaha attempted to win the prestigious Gold Cup. Over two and a half miles of hilly British turf, the colt battled with the filly Quashed, only to be defeated in a photo finish. In *American Race Horses of 1936*, historian John Hervey wrote a chapter entitled "Omaha Abroad" and described the Gold Cup as follows:

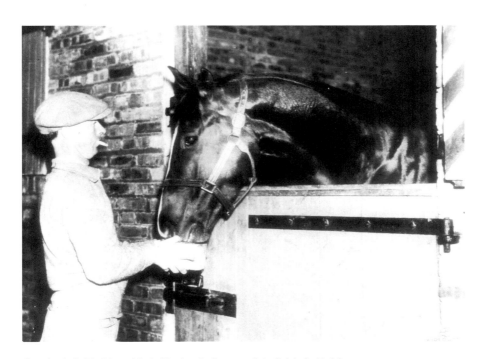

Omaha is fed in his stable in England. *Courtesy of the Belair Stable Museum.*

Such a spectacle at the end of a 2½ mile race had not been seen at Ascot in so many years that the excitement and suspense became overpowering. Everything else was forgotten as the immense crowd in spellbound silence watched the two horses racing to them with victory impossible to predict until the post was reached. They were now but 100 yards from the finish and the strain upon the spectators had become almost unbearable.

The judges' verdict decided the destination of the stakes and bets, but everyone who saw the race will, for all time, regard the honors as equally divided.[31]

Following the Gold Cup loss, Team Omaha encountered subsequent disappointment at Newmarket, when the colt lost the Princess of Wales Stakes by a neck to the Aga Khan's Taj Akbar. Sweating profusely, the American champion carried 138 pounds, 18 more than the eventual winner. Shortly after this race, Omaha injured his left foreleg while training and was shipped back to the United States to begin stud duty at Claiborne Farm.

Regrettably, Omaha was not a success at stud, as the Belair Bullet was fruitless in producing stakes winners. As a result, in 1943, Woodward leased Omaha to the Jockey Club's Lookover Stallion Station in Avon, New York. In 1950, the horse was purchased by a group of breeders and sent to his namesake of Omaha, Nebraska. For a twenty-five-dollar donation to charity, owners could breed their mares to the Triple Crown champion. During the following years, the Belair Bullet developed somewhat of a cult following, serving as a mascot at Nebraska's Ak-Sar Ben Racetrack. In later years, he was often photographed with young children perched upon his back as a handler fed treats to the aging champion. According to the *Journal of Kentucky History and Genealogy*, "When the gate bell rang to begin a race, the old campaigner would lift his head and lope forward down the track inside the rail (to the delight of the fans), as if reliving his glory days from decades ago."[32]

Omaha lived a long life, succumbing to the infirmities of old age at twenty-seven. In remembering the great champion, the *Daily Racing Form* penned the following: "In action he was a glorious sight; few thoroughbreds have exhibited such a magnificent, sweeping, space-annihilating stride, or carried it with such strength and precision. His place is among the Titans of the American turf."[33]

Omaha was buried in the Circle of Champions at the Ak-Sar-Ben racetrack, which also held a race named in his honor. When the track closed in 1995, the land was purchased by the University of Nebraska–Omaha.

Cradle of Maryland Horse Racing

According to urban legend, Omaha's remains are situated alongside a culinary arts classroom, and the late champion is often called upon by students for good luck. Other sources assert, however, that the exact location of his remains is unknown, as construction occurred when the racetrack was closed and it is likely that Omaha's bones were moved.

Omaha's sweep of the Triple Crown races earned Belair a prominent place in history. At the very moment Omaha crossed the finish line at Belmont, Belair became the only owner/breeder to produce father-son Triple Crown champions. As of this writing, that feat has yet to be duplicated.

The wins of Gallant Fox and Omaha were far from lucky coincidences. Rather, these victories resulted from decades of careful planning and breeding by William Woodward. Devoted to his research of bloodlines, Woodward was patient in developing lines that provided the distance and stamina that would win classic races. Woodward's horses were bred for substance, and many possessed the conformation that would withstand a rigorous Fitzsimmons training and racing schedule. Most of all, Woodward hoped, they would produce a winner of the Epsom Derby.

Chapter 9

OTHER BELAIR FAVORITES

As America labored through the years of the Great Depression, Belair Stud prospered in what was to be its finest decade. In addition to Gallant Fox and Omaha, William Woodward raced several other classic winners in the 1930s and well into the 1940s, both in the United States and abroad. While it is impossible to discuss all of the Belair stakes winners within the scope of several chapters, a few of the most popular are highlighted on these pages.

FAIRENO

In 1932, nestled snugly between the wins of Gallant Fox and Omaha, Belair Stud boasted its second Belmont Stakes winner, Faireno. Foaled at Claiborne Farm in 1929, the bay colt was sired by Chatterton, a son of Fair Play (who also sired Man o' War) out of the mare Minerva. Faireno had some success as a two-year-old, carrying the Belair silks to wins in the Victoria Stakes at Woodbine Racetrack in Canada, the Nursery Handicap at Belmont Park and the Junior Champion Stakes at Aqueduct.

As Faireno's three-year-old season started out poorly, Woodward opted not to run him in the Kentucky Derby. The horse was shipped to Pimlico in May but did not race in the Preakness, instead returning to Mr. Fitz's stable at Aqueduct for further training. In preparation for the Belmont Stakes, the colt was entered in the Campfire Purse at Belmont, where he finished a strong second. This pre-Belmont strategy proved to be successful, as Faireno led virtually wire-to-wire in winning the Belmont Stakes for Belair.

Following his victory at Belmont, Faireno returned to Aqueduct, where he was triumphant in the Shevlin Stakes. On July 2, he soared to victory in the Dwyer Stakes, but that win was followed by a dismal showing in the Arlington Classic, in which he finished eighth. Faireno rebounded in August, winning the Hawthorne Handicap and placing a strong second behind Plucky Play in the Hawthorne Gold Cup. On September 17, he added a win in the Lawrence Realization but sustained a tendon injury that would sideline him for more than a year. Nevertheless, at season's end, Faireno shared champion three-year-old male honors with Kentucky Derby champion Burgoo King.

Rested for his entire four-year-old season, Faireno returned to the track at age five, making his debut at Jamaica in the Paumonok Handicap. While he gave the race his best effort, Faireno tired in the stretch and ultimately finished fourth. He soon returned to championship form, however, winning the Empire City Handicap, the Havre de Grace Handicap, the Merchants and Citizens Handicap at Saratoga and the Rochambeau Handicap at Narragansett Race Track. In the Havre de Grace, Faireno defeated the great Discovery, the horse who would later deny Omaha Horse of the Year honors. After only modest success as a six-year-old, Faireno retired to stud but, disappointingly, was found to be sterile.

GRANVILLE

Another key winner in the 1930s for Belair was the colt Granville, a son of Gallant Fox out of the mare Gravita. Granville's juvenile season was disappointing, and he won only one of his seven starts. His best finish was a third-place showing in the 1935 Champagne Stakes at Belmont, a race that was won by Joseph Widener's colt, Brevity.

Showing promise in his three-year-old season, Granville finished second in a photo finish behind the Phipps colt, Teufel, in the Wood Memorial. Hopes were high for the son of Gallant Fox in the Kentucky Derby; however, in a stroke of unfortunate luck, he stumbled and fell to his knees in the early moments of the race, tossing jockey James Stout and forcing his own elimination from the Run for the Roses. After losing the Preakness by a nose to the Derby champion, Bold Venture, Granville found a stroke of good fortune, defeating Dwyer Stakes champion Mr. Bones by a nose in a thrilling Belmont Stakes finish.

Above: Granville with jockey James Stout. *Courtesy of the Belair Stable Museum.*

Left: Jockey James Stout (left) and William Woodward (center) accept Granville's Saratoga Cup trophy from George Bull. *Courtesy of the Belair Stable Museum.*

Following the Belmont victory, Granville won a series of races for Belair; these included the 1¼-mile Arlington Classic in Chicago, as well as both the Kenner and the Travers at Saratoga. In the 1¾-mile Saratoga Cup, Granville defeated the aforementioned Discovery by eight lengths in what was both literally and figuratively a two-horse race. Granville capped off this win with a victory in the 1⅝-mile Lawrence Realization Stakes, proving that he was indeed a distance horse.

In eleven starts as a three-year-old, Granville amassed seven wins and three seconds, earning championship honors as the top three-year-old colt. When formal voting was implemented by the *Daily Racing Form* in 1936, Granville became the first horse to be voted Horse of the Year. At the end of his championship season, however, Granville sustained an ankle injury, which led to his retirement. Unfortunately, he did not stamp his offspring with talent and was ultimately disappointing as a sire.

Fighting Fox and Foxbrough

In 1935, excitement was high at Claiborne Farm with the arrival of Fighting Fox, a full brother to Gallant Fox. While the colt would not duplicate his brother's Triple Crown success, Fighting Fox would win several key stakes races for Belair. As a two-year-old, his record included a win in Saratoga's Grand Union Hotel Stakes and solid third-place finishes in the Futurity, Hopeful and Champagne Stakes. Fighting Fox won the Wood Memorial in his three-year-old season and, among other in-the-money finishes, placed third in both the Travers and the Whitney. He raced through the age of five, winning several handicaps (including the Massachusetts, Carter, Fleetwing, Jamaica and Wilmington races) at the age of four and capturing the Paumonok Handicap in his final season.

Another full brother to Gallant Fox, the colt Foxbrough (also known as Foxbrough II) was foaled in 1936. Racing abroad as a juvenile, Foxbrough was named champion two-year-old colt in England and was an early favorite for the Epsom Derby. Regrettably, he was forced to withdraw due to an injury. Foxbrough returned to the United States, where his wins included the Butler and the Yonkers handicap races.

Opposite, top: Fighting Fox (James Stout, up), full brother to Gallant Fox, shown here at Aqueduct in 1939. *Courtesy of the Belair Stable Museum.*

Opposite, bottom: Foxbrough, full brother to Gallant Fox, at Aqueduct in 1941. *Courtesy of the Belair Stable Museum.*

JOHNSTOWN

Belair's success continued in the late 1930s with the Arthur Hancock–bred colt Johnstown. Foaled at Claiborne Farm in 1936, Johnstown was sired by multiple stakes winner Jamestown out of the mare La France, a daughter of Sir Gallahad III. Affectionately nicknamed "Big John" by the racing media, the large bay was privately purchased as a yearling by Woodward for Belair.

Johnstown gained early success as a two-year-old, winning seven of his twelve starts. Ridden by Belair's regular jockey James Stout, Johnstown began his classic season with a smashing victory in the Wood Memorial— one year after stable mate Fighting Fox had captured the same race. Johnstown's win in the Wood made him the favorite for the Kentucky Derby, and the colt, known for his "lop ears," made the race his own. Following a difficult start, Johnstown surged to the lead at the mile pole, besting eventual horse of the year Challedon by a stunning eight lengths. *Time* magazine later noted that, in the Derby, Johnstown "made all his contemporaries look like hobby horses."[34]

Johnstown with jockey James Stout and William Woodward. *Courtesy of the Belair Stable Museum.*

With the seemingly easy defeat of Challedon, Johnstown was anointed by racing media as the greatest horse since Man o' War. Heading into the Preakness Stakes, Big John faced a new challenge; heavy rains had saturated the Pimlico track, and Johnstown would face deep mud footing for the first time in his career. After leading well into the backstretch, Johnstown faded to fifth in the stretch as Challedon rallied to win by a length and a half over Gilded Knight. Then it was off to the Belmont, where the Belair colt relished the added distance. In the absence of his key rival Challedon, who was not eligible for the race, Johnstown topped the field of six starters in an easy triumph over Belay. He followed this win with victories in the Dwyer and Withers before falling to Challedon in the Arlington Classic. With this loss, Johnstown became widely recognized as a horse who would win two out of every three races.

At the end of the 1939 season, Johnstown was retired to Claiborne Farm with career earnings of $169,315. While he produced only 6 stakes winners out of 227 foals, Johnstown became a leading broodmare sire. Johnstown died in 1950 at the age of fourteen and was buried in the equine cemetery at Claiborne Farm.

Bolstered in part by Johnstown's success, William Woodward was named the sport's leading owner in 1939. That same year, Woodward was featured on the cover of *Time* magazine, which profiled the master of Belair in an article entitled "Scarlet Spots."

VAGRANCY

Foaled in 1939 by Sir Gallahad III out of the mare Valkyr (by Man o' War), the bay filly Vagrancy was one of Belair's most prolific winners in the 1940s. Known as Sunny Jim Fitzsimmons's "favorite filly," she raced forty-two times, finishing in the money in thirty-one of her starts and winning many of the most prestigious stakes races for fillies at that time.

Vagrancy was widely revered for her grit on the track as she took on both males and older horses. The filly earned praise when she placed second behind Preakness champion Alsab in the Lawrence Realization Stakes. That season, she won nine stakes races, including the Coaching Club American, Pimlico and Delaware Oaks, as well as the Alabama, Gazelle and Test Stakes against her own age. She also topped older fillies and mares in the Beldame and Ladies Handicap races.

Above: Vagrancy wins at Belmont Park in 1942. *Courtesy of the Belair Stable Museum.*

Left: Belair's Bossuet was part of the first triple dead heat in history at the 1944 Carter Handicap. *Courtesy of the Belair Stable Museum.*

With a hefty purse of $18,000, the Beldame was the richest race of the Aqueduct meet that day. The importance of the race was heralded by the *New York Times*, which wrote: "The place of honor [on the race card] is for the Beldame, which aids the breeding of the sport by encouraging the development of good race mares." Leading for the majority of the race, Vagrancy was met at the wire by Bing Crosby and Lin Howard's Barrancosa for a photo finish. The *New York Times* reported on the "dead heat" race, noting that William Woodward "flipped a coin in the unsaddling enclosure after the finish and thereby lost possession for the coming year of the Beldame Trophy." (Interestingly, Belair would also finish as part of the first triple dead heat in history in 1944, when Woodward's homebred Bossuet joined two other horses at the wire in the Carter Handicap at Aqueduct.)

Vagrancy finished the season strong, capturing Champion Three-Year-Old Filly and Champion Handicap Mare honors. Retiring to broodmare duty for Belair, Vagrancy would produce three stakes winners, including the fillies Vulcania and Natasha. Perhaps her most famous offspring, the colt Black Tarquin, would bring William Woodward an important English classic win.

The Vagrancy Handicap, a race for fillies and mares ages three and up, was established in her honor in 1948 at Aqueduct and is currently run at Belmont Park.

ENGLISH CHAMPIONS

While Belair horses continued to dominate the U.S. racing scene, they also won several key races in England. In 1930 and 1931, William Woodward won back-to-back winnings of the Newmarket Stakes with two sons of Sir Gallahad III: the Scout II and Sir Andrew. The latter, out of the mare Gravitate, was named as a tribute to Belair's faithful employee, Andrew Jackson, whom Woodward described as his "most trusted advisor in all things equine." In addition to naming a horse in his honor, Woodward was so fond of, and grateful to, Jackson that he penned and published an oral history entitled *Andrew Jackson, Africanus*. When Jackson passed away in 1932, Woodward purchased a headstone that read: "Andrew Jackson; died March 18, 1932 at Belair. In affectionate memory of a long and faithful service." The headstone still stands near Belair at Sacred Heart Church.

In 1933, Belair boasted its first British classic winner in the filly Brown Betty. The stunning, seal brown filly was purchased for Woodward by his

Portrait of Brown Betty, Belair's first English classic winner. *Courtesy of the Belair Stable Museum.*

English trainer Cecil Boyd-Rochfort for the small sum of 1,600 guineas. According to the UK's National Horse Racing Museum, the English trainer and American owner had "fallen in love with" the filly "when they saw her silhouetted against the sky at Sir Alec Black's stud farm." Brown Betty's appearance also earned praise from several other horsemen; one renowned French trainer allegedly referred to her as "the best looking filly [he] had ever seen."

Named affectionately for Boyd-Rochfort's niece Betty McCall, the filly possessed more than just striking good looks; she was also a talented runner. Brown Betty raced well as a two-year-old, winning the Cheveley Park Stakes and placing second in both the Molecombe Stakes and Chesterfield Stakes in 1932. The following year, she became the first English classic winner for both Boyd-Rochfort and Woodward when she topped the 1,000 Guineas at Newmarket. The race, inaugurated in 1814, was one of the two classic races restricted to three-year-old fillies. After failing to finish in the top three in the longer-distance Oaks, Brown Betty was shipped to Belair, where she produced two stakes-winning foals.

Three years after Brown Betty's win in the 1,000 Guineas, Woodward captured his second English classic, the St. Leger Stakes at Doncaster. The winner was Boswell, a colt by Bosworth out of the Sir Gallahad mare Flying Gal. Ridden by jockey Pat Beasley, Boswell shocked the British crowds by defeating the favorites, which included the popular Rhodes Scholar, in a thrilling victory over one and three-quarter miles.

In the same season in which Boswell won the St. Leger, another Belair colt, Flares, also earned success in England. Flares, foaled in 1933, was a full brother to Omaha. However, unlike his brother, who began his career in the United States, Flares was sent to England as a yearling to train with Boyd-Rochfort. The results were outstanding, and in May 1936, three-year-old Flares won the Newmarket Stakes. The following season, he won a series of distance races. The colt topped the Princess of Wales Stakes at a mile and a half, followed by the mile-and-a-quarter Champion Stakes and the Lowther Stakes over a mile and three-quarters.

The following season, at odds of 100 to 7, Flares avenged his brother's loss in the Ascot Gold Cup. The attractive colt stunned bettors, becoming the first American horse since Foxhall (in 1882) to capture the two-and-a-half-mile race. Following this victory, Flares returned to the United States as a breeding stallion; his offspring would include Chop Chop, a five-time leading sire in Canada, and Epigram, winner of the 1952 Queen's Plate.

As he drew closer to his goal of winning the Epsom Derby, William Woodward earned his third English classic win with the victory of Hycilla in the 1944 Epsom Oaks. The chestnut filly was foaled in 1941, having been bred by Woodward in Ireland. She was sired by the Epsom Derby champion Hyperion out of Belair's homebred mare, Priscilla Carter. As the latter was an American-bred, Hycilla herself was considered a "half-bred" and was thus deemed ineligible for the General Stud Book. In 1944, Hycilla won two stakes races for Belair, capturing top honors in both the Oaks and Champion Stakes. After initially being favored in the St. Leger, Hycilla faded and failed to place. At that point, the filly was shipped home to Belair, where she produced four minor stakes winners.

Woodward's success abroad continued in the following years, as he won his fourth English classic with Black Tarquin in 1948. As a two-year-old, the large, seal brown son of Vagrancy capped off several victories, including the historic Gimcrack and Royal Lodge Stakes. His wins at age three included the Derby Trial and St. James's Palace, and he earned the third British classic

Flares wins the Ascot Gold Cup. *Courtesy of the Belair Stable Museum.*

victory for Belair when he won the St. Leger Stakes. At season's end, Black Tarquin was named England's champion three-year-old colt, demonstrating his talent at various distances. The near-black colt continued to race at age four, winning the Chippenham, Burwell and White Rose Stakes and placing second in the Gold Cup at Ascot. Retiring after his four-year-old season, Black Tarquin was sent to stand at Claiborne Farm and was subsequently shipped to Ireland.

William Woodward had amassed an impressive number of stakes winnings, and his horses had carried the Belair silks to numerous classic victories, both in the United States and abroad. By 1950, however, Woodward's health had begun to decline, and appearances at his beloved racetracks became far less frequent. Weakened by the lingering effects of heart disease, Woodward began preparations to pass along the proverbial torch of Belair Stud. He retired from his position at the Jockey Club and assigned many of his racing duties to his only son, Billy.

Billy Woodward was gifted with an enviable combination of dashing good looks and a hefty trust fund. Standing over six feet tall, Billy's slim build and handsome face gave him the appearance of a matinee idol. He was highly educated, having been registered at Groton at the time of his birth. Like his father, Billy had graduated from Harvard University and eventually became a director at the Hanover Bank. Prior to his career in banking, Billy had served time in the U.S. Navy, earning a medal for bravery during World War II.

While Billy shared his father's interests in education and banking, he had little enthusiasm for the sport of horse racing. In the coming months and years, however, that was about to change. The reluctant Billy Woodward was about to become master of Belair.

Chapter 10

A CHANGING OF THE GUARDS

On May 27, 1950, the aging William Woodward watched on television from home as his colt, Prince Simon, was led to the track for the Epsom Derby. With his health quickly failing, Woodward held close to his lifelong dream of winning the Derby. Prince Simon, a bay colt by the champion Princequillo, was wildly favored in the race. In fact, the horse had so impressed Cecil Boyd-Rochfort that the trainer had cabled Woodward with the enthusiastic words:"I think he is perhaps one of the best you have ever had, and you may have the animal you have always longed for."[35]

Tall and long-strided, Prince Simon appeared destined for victory as he galloped, almost effortlessly, along Epsom's storied turf. Suddenly, at the very moment that victory beckoned, Prince Simon was bested by a head by the French horse Galcador. Prince Simon, named England's top Thoroughbred of 1950, would be forever regarded as "the best horse never to have won the Derby." Perhaps fortunately for Woodward, he did not experience this disappointment in person, as illness had forced him to forego the trip to England. In Woodward's place was the reluctant Billy, who attended the race out of respect for his father's wishes. Billy was also encouraged to attend the races by his glamorous wife, Ann, who enjoyed the pageantry of the sport of kings.

Born Angeline Crowell in rural Kansas, Ann Woodward first met her future husband at a swanky New York nightclub in 1942. Desperate to achieve success as an actress, she had changed her name to the more alluring Ann Eden for work as a chorus girl, dancer and model. Ann had a stint on the radio show *Joyce Jordan, Girl Interne*, for which she was dubbed the "most beautiful girl in radio." Despite their obvious differences in class, Ann and Billy began a torrid romance. Ann's earthiness and fiery temper attracted the conservative Billy, who was bored with the endless string of debutantes he had previously courted.

On one of their early dates, Billy had brought Ann to Saratoga, where the Woodward family watched the Belair horse Apache win the Empire City Handicap. It was there

Billy and Ann Woodward. *Courtesy of the Belair Stable Museum.*

that Ann was originally introduced to Elsie Woodward. From first glance, Elsie appeared to dislike Ann, believing that the young showgirl's meager background was unbefitting a Woodward. Ignoring his mother's obvious disdain, Billy continued courting Ann, spending large amounts of time at her New York apartment. The two shared a passionate romance, calling each other by the pet names of "Monk" and "Dunk," which were derived from a whimsical painting that was displayed in Ann's apartment.

While stationed with the U.S. Navy in Tacoma, Washington, Billy proposed to Ann, and the two married in 1943. The young couple settled into married life, becoming parents to two sons: William III (Woody), born in 1945, and James (Jimmy), who arrived two years later.

By the spring of 1953, as William Sr.'s health continued to fail, Billy had assumed many of his father's Belair responsibilities. One crisp morning, Billy joined Mr. Fitz in walking the paddocks to determine which yearlings would carry the Belair colors. As the young master of Belair walked alongside one of the paddocks, a handsome mahogany bay yearling bucked and trotted toward him.

The colt was Nashua, the result of generations of careful breeding by William Woodward Sr. The colt was a son of the Irish stallion Nasrullah, who had been imported to the United States by Arthur Hancock and a

Above: Nasrullah, sire of Nashua. *Courtesy of the Keeneland Library.*

Left: William Woodward displaying his sense of humor. *Courtesy of the Belair Stable Museum.*

syndicate that included the elder Woodward. Nasrullah was well regarded as a highly talented horse but one whose volatile temperament had stood as a roadblock on the path to success. Nasrullah had a mind of his own and often chose to fight his jockey rather than give his all in a race. Nevertheless, he showed success as a breeding stallion; in 1950, Nasrullah's Irish-bred son, Noor, defeated the great Citation in four successive stakes races. Nashua's dam, Segula, had also demonstrated some success on the track. A daughter of Johnstown, Segula had won nine races in forty-nine starts and had finished third in the Coaching Club American Oaks. While there is no proof of the definitive origins of Nashua's name, it is likely that Woodward derived it from his days at Groton, remembering the Nashua River that flowed nearby.

William Woodward Sr. had viewed Nashua when the colt was a weanling and was highly impressed with the young horse's sturdy build and strong legs. Woodward's plans were to send Nashua to England to train under Boyd-Rochfort for the English classic races. With the master of Belair's health quickly failing, Nashua was Woodward's last hope to win the English Derby.

Sadly, Woodward's dream of winning the Derby would never come to fruition. On September 25, 1953, William Woodward Sr. passed away at his home in New York. His estate would be shared among his wife and five children, with the racing operations left entirely to his only son. Woodward's last will and testament bequeathed the Belair estate to Billy, with the hope that the farm "may mean as much to my son as it has to my uncle and myself, and that he may spend many happy days there."[36]

The entire racing world mourned the death of Woodward Sr., whose contributions to the sport of kings had been nothing less than monumental. In the weeks that followed, the Maryland Jockey Club established the Woodward Purse in his honor, to be run on the undercard of the Pimlico Futurity. The next year, the Woodward Stakes was established at Aqueduct. Befitting the man for whom it was named, the Woodward Stakes would become one of the nation's premier stakes races in the years to come.

Chapter 11

NASHUA THE GREAT

On May 5, 1954, less than one year after William Woodward Sr.'s death, Nashua made his racing debut. The race was held at New York's historic Belmont Park, far from the courses in England that Woodward Sr. had targeted for the handsome colt. After the elder Woodward's death, Billy had closed Belair's English operations, opting instead to focus on the elite U.S. racing circuit. Nashua would begin his racing career over four and a half furlongs under the watchful eye of Sunny Jim Fitzsimmons.

In a field of twenty-one maidens, the attractive bay colt showed impressive form. Nashua broke from post position fourteen, with Mr. Fitz's regular rider Jess Higley poised squarely in the saddle. Nashua, whom Fitzsimmons nicknamed "Mickey" due to his Irish heritage, made the race look easy, besting the field by three lengths in a time of 0:52 $^3/_5$.

In the starting gate next to Nashua was the colt Golden Prince, ridden by jockey Eddie Arcaro. Known in racing circles as "the Master," Arcaro's smooth riding style had earned him numerous accolades. He was the first and only jockey to win two Triple Crowns, guiding the immortal Whirlaway and Citation into the annals of history. Gifted with a keen eye and intelligence beyond his years, Arcaro saw early brilliance in Nashua. He later told *Sports Illustrated*:

> *The first time I saw Nashua—or at least the first time I can remember seeing him—I had better than a clubhouse seat. The occasion was a four-and-a-half furlong maiden race at Belmont Park almost exactly a year ago,*

on May 5, 1954. I was on Mrs. L. Lazare's Golden Prince, breaking from post position 13. Next to me in 14 was Jess Higley on Nashua. During the race I had problems enough of my own, but I still have a vivid recollection of Nashua turning on a wonderful burst of speed and winning easily by three lengths. My horse finished 11th.

Sometimes a jockey can see qualities in a horse that make him immediately want to ride that horse in future races. I have had such a "second sense" about horses before this—with Assault and Citation, for instance. In Nashua's case I knew instinctively as he drew away from his field that this was a horse with a determined will to win.[37]

After the race, Arcaro approached Fitzsimmons to inquire about the prospect of gaining the mount on Nashua. A deal was made, and a great partnership commenced. While the jockey would sometimes publicly state his frustrations with Nashua's various quirks, Arcaro and the colt shared a winning partnership. Later, in the spring of 1955, Arcaro would have nothing but praise for Nashua in an article for *Sports Illustrated* entitled "Nashua: That Horse I Ride—Wow!"

Nashua works under Eddie Arcaro. *Courtesy of Russ Davies.*

Arcaro's first race aboard the strapping son of Nasrullah came just one short week after Nashua's debut. In the five-furlong Juvenile Stakes at Belmont Park, Nashua would face the horse who was to become his primary rival. Summer Tan, a precocious bay colt owned by Dorothy Firestone, was to challenge Nashua on various occasions. However, Nashua took top honors in this first meeting of the two, besting his new rival in a one-and-a-half-length win.

Mr. Fitz was known for racing his horses frequently, and Nashua's schedule was no different. One week after the Juvenile Stakes, Nashua headed to New Jersey for the five-furlong Cherry Hill Stakes at Garden State. As Arcaro was serving a brief suspension, Jess Higley returned for the ride on Nashua. The big bay was sent off as the second betting choice, with Royal Note—another colt previously ridden by Arcaro—deemed the odds-on favorite. In this race, Nashua showed his tendency to "prop," or slow down once he had gained the lead. Despite urging from Higley, Nashua lost by a head to Royal Note, ultimately finishing five lengths ahead of the third-place finisher.

Nashua had a bit of a rest before heading to Saratoga for the summer races. On August 21, with Arcaro back on board, Nashua made his first attempt at six furlongs in the Spa's Grand Union Hotel Stakes. Again, "Mickey" was sent off as the second betting choice, with C.V. Whitney's Pyranees deemed the favorite at post time. This race marked the first in which Nashua was equipped with blinkers; the colt would wear them on an on-again, off-again basis throughout his career. Once again, Arcaro was victorious with Nashua, winning the race by $1\,^3/_4$ lengths in a time of $1:12\,^2/_5$.

One week after the win, Nashua returned to the Spa's hallowed dirt track for the six-and-a-half-furlong Hopeful Stakes. The premier summer race for two-year-olds, the Hopeful boasted an impressive list of past winners that included the likes of Whirlaway and Man o' War. In a field of eight juveniles that included Summer Tan, Nashua was favored for the first time in his career. Breaking well from the gate, Nashua led wire to wire as he thwarted various challengers. He completed the race in $1:17\,^4/_5$, which was within $^4/_5$ of the existing track record and marked the first Hopeful victory for Jim Fitzsimmons.

Three weeks after the Hopeful, Nashua returned to Fitz's home base at Aqueduct for the Cowdin Stakes. There he would reunite with rival Summer Tan for a duel over six and a half furlongs. Nashua, carrying top weight of 124 pounds, was sent off as the favorite. Carrying 4 fewer pounds than Nashua, Summer Tan won this round of the battle, setting a track record in the process.

Eddie Arcaro aboard Nashua in Florida. *Courtesy of the National Racing Museum and Hall of Fame.*

On the heels of this defeat, Nashua headed back to Belmont for the six-furlong Anticipation Purse. This race was to serve as the colt's prep for the upcoming Futurity, which would also take place at Belmont Park. Nashua proved he was ready for the challenge, and did so impressively, winning by a length over Royal Coinage and equaling the existing track record of 1:08 ^{1}/$_5$. This victory solidified Nashua's status as the favorite for the Futurity, and he would carry high weight of 122 pounds. As expected, the Futurity came down to a thrilling duel between Nashua and Summer Tan, with Nashua ultimately winning by a head. As this was the first Futurity victory for the legendary Jim Fitzsimmons, a special trophy was created commemorating the event. *Sports Illustrated*, in response to this victory, proclaimed Nashua "the horse to watch."

While there was speculation that Nashua would next run in the Garden State Stakes, Billy Woodward announced that the colt would forego the race. Rather, Nashua would be heading to Belair for a brief period of rest and relaxation. The horse had apparently suffered from a touch of a virus, and

Woodward was not about to take any chances with his big horse. In Nashua's absence, Summer Tan virtually annihilated the competition, winning by an astounding nine lengths. Nevertheless, Nashua had completed his two-year-old season with a record of six wins and two seconds in eight starts; with earnings of $192,865, he was named champion two-year-old colt.

While Billy Woodward had not initially shared his father's passion for racing, Nashua's success had ignited a spark deep within him. The younger Woodward developed a genuine excitement for the sport and a heartfelt appreciation for his magnificent horse. Billy, dressed impeccably in a crisp dark suit and "lucky" striped tie, enjoyed leading Nashua to frequent winner's circle ceremonies. He often rose early to observe Nashua's workouts and walked the track to assess the footing before key races. Billy's pride in Nashua was enormously apparent, as he was often observed affectionately petting the great horse's neck.

After a four-month layoff in which Nashua grew in height and girth, the horse began his three-year-old season in mid-February at Florida's Hialeah Park. The race was the Spanish Moss Purse, and it was a time of firsts for the

Billy Woodward and Nashua (Eddie Arcaro, up). *Courtesy of the Belair Stable Museum.*

temperamental colt. The distance of $1^1/_{16}$ miles would be Nashua's longest thus far, and he would carry the classic race weight of 126 pounds. Again, the colt showed no resistance to the added distance or weight and, with Arcaro in the saddle, won his three-year-old debut. On February 26, the pair returned to the track for the nine-furlong Flamingo Stakes. The favorite at odds of 7–10, the sturdy Nashua battled eleven other horses over Hialeah's dirt track. Under urging by Arcaro's whip, Nashua won the Flamingo by one and a half lengths, sealing his position as a favorite for the upcoming Kentucky Derby.

Next up for Nashua was the $1^1/_8$-mile Florida Derby, another key prep for the Run for the Roses. Heavy rains had rendered the track a field of slop, and trainer Jim Fitzsimmons, at home nursing a cold, pondered the idea of scratching the valuable colt. Such deep mud could be problematic for a young horse, and Mr. Fitz did not want to risk a serious injury.

While Fitz recuperated at home, Billy Woodward walked the track with Eddie Arcaro to assess the situation. During the process, Billy was amazed at the number of fans who had braved the weather to see Nashua run. When it was determined that the footing was safe, Billy made the decision that Nashua would indeed race. Too many fans had been looking forward to seeing the Belair colt, and Woodward did not want to disappoint them. Nashua ultimately handled the footing well, winning by two lengths over First Cabin. To the media, Billy Woodward's decision propelled him into the role of a national sports hero.

On April 23, Nashua ran his final Derby prep race, the Wood Memorial at Jamaica. Once again, the race was a showdown between Nashua and Summer Tan, with the latter coming off a spectacular victory in his seasonal debut. Summer Tan had earned the sympathy of the racing public when he was stricken with a near-fatal intestinal embolism the previous autumn. The horse beat the odds and not only recovered but proved his mettle in a fourteen-length debut win. The question remained, however, as to whether he would be well enough to overtake Nashua.

With Arcaro serving another suspension, Ted Atkinson gained the ride on Nashua for the Wood Memorial. Atkinson, who had breezed Nashua in the past, had what many described as a "hustling, punishing style" that some believed would benefit the sometimes lazy colt in the stretch. Nashua was sent off as the 6–5 second choice, with the heroic Summer Tan deemed the favorite at 3–5 odds.

The strong competition between the colts was at an all-time high, and, as the gates opened, the two set off on a $1^1/_8$-mile duel. In the end it was

Billy and Ann Woodward with Nashua (Eddie Arcaro, up). *Courtesy of the Belair Stable Museum.*

Atkinson on Nashua who prevailed, besting Eric Guerin and Summer Tan by a neck at the wire. By now, the rivalry had gained the attention of the hungry media, who predicted a thrilling showdown at Churchill Downs for the first Saturday in May. It was a prediction that was shared by fans and trainers alike, including Sunny Jim and the rest of "Team Nashua." In fact, many were so focused on Summer Tan that they failed to take notice of another Derby-bound colt—a chestnut California-bred by the name of Swaps.

While Nashua was hailed as the "blueblood" from the East, Swaps was the "cowboy horse" from the West. Bred in the desert of California, the lanky chestnut was owned by Rex Ellsworth, a former cowhand. Ellsworth and his trainer, Meshach "Mesh" Tenney, had an unorthodox "western" training style that differed from the traditional methods of the East. As such, the pair was often not taken seriously in elite racing circles.

Despite his unusual background, Swaps showed that he could win big races. The colt had begun his classic season with a three-and-a-half-length win in the San Vicente Stakes, which he followed with a clear victory in the Santa Anita Stakes. Nevertheless, with the media squarely focused on the Nashua–Summer Tan rivalry, Swaps was not viewed by many as a legitimate threat. He finally gained some attention in his last prep for the Kentucky Derby, when he catapulted to victory by eight and a half lengths under the twin spires in the Jefferson Purse. By Derby Day, the western visitor was sent off as the second betting choice, with Nashua, the eastern champ, deemed the odds-on favorite.

When the gates opened on Derby Day, Swaps raced to a customary early lead under the young but talented jockey Willie Shoemaker. As Fitzsimmons's instructions to Eddie Arcaro had been to keep a solid eye on Summer Tan, Arcaro did not initially challenge Swaps. "I let Shoemaker have an easy lead, with nobody bothering him," Arcaro later recalled. With the jockey's energy squarely focused on Summer Tan, Swaps opened up his lead, and despite a noble stretch run, Nashua was unable to catch him. Swaps won the race by a length and a half over Nashua, who was a full six and a half lengths ahead of Summer Tan. "If you could rerun it, I'd have run up and got Swaps," Arcaro lamented. "At least I'd have run up to him in the middle of the backstretch and made him go to running."[38]

Nashua's loss in the Kentucky Derby was a stinging blow to Billy Woodward, who replayed the race over and over in his mind. It was the same for Arcaro and Fitzsimmons, with each man blaming himself for the upset. The octogenarian Jim Fitzsimmons, hunched by a combination of age and arthritis, later told *Sports Illustrated*:

> *Nashua did not lose the Derby because of any fault of his. He lost it because I chucked it for him with my instructions to Eddie Arcaro to watch Summer Tan. I didn't know much about this horse Swaps, but a few fellows who thought they did told me they figured him for a mile or a mile-and-a-furlong horse—in other words one who probably wouldn't like the mile-and-a-quarter Derby distance. I was wrong to believe it. In that race we lay back—as it turned out we lay back too far—watching Summer Tan while Swaps did the first three-quarters in an easy 1:12 ²/₅. When Eddie finally saw Summer Tan was not going to be the threat that I had said he would be, he went after Swaps. It was no use. Swaps had a good finishing kick, and we were cleanly licked. We had no excuse. I've never alibied for any loss and never will. But I figured I chucked that race, and I felt all along that things might be different if the two horses ever met again.*[39]

Ever the gracious sportsman, the disappointed Billy Woodward immediately congratulated Swaps's owner, Rex Ellsworth. According to sources, Billy also mentioned the prospect of the two horses meeting in a match race sometime in the future. With Swaps heading back out west and Nashua taking on the Preakness Stakes, that possibility would remain to be seen.

Chapter 12

TRIUMPH AND TRAGEDY

With his Derby upset now squarely behind him, Nashua headed to Pimlico for the second jewel in horse racing's Triple Crown. The Belair colt returned to championship form in the Preakness, winning the race in a record time of 1:54.3. In early June, Nashua carried the Belair silks to a sixth Belmont Stakes win, dominating the rest of the field by an electrifying nine lengths. It was then off to Aqueduct, where only two others opted to face Nashua in the Dwyer Stakes—and they were unable to outrun him. After adding the Dwyer to his list of wins, Nashua captured the Arlington Classic in Chicago, where he narrowly defeated the game Traffic Judge by a half length for the win. The lasting popularity of Belair was apparent at Arlington Park, as a mural displayed a photograph of William Woodward Sr. leading a Belair horse.

While Nashua continued to demonstrate winning form in the East, Swaps was taking California by storm. Among the Derby champion's eight straight victories were an impressive twelve-length win in the Will Rogers Stakes and world record–setting performances in the California Stakes and the American Derby. As a result, the media and racing public clamored for a rematch between the two colts. The media focused on a battle between the rivals, polling attendees at the annual Belmont Ball for their thoughts on who would win if the two colts were to meet again. Among many responses, Robert Strawbridge Jr., president of the Coaching Club of America, replied with the following: "Nashua. He is getting better all the time. With the lone exception of the Kentucky Derby, he has shown improvement in every race.

THE BELMONT
BELMONT PARK .. $100,000 ADDED .. JUNE 11, 1955
BELAIR STUD'S NASHUA EDDIE ARCARO up
J. FITZSIMMONS trainer 1112 Miles Time 2:29
BLAZING COUNT 2nd PORTERSVILLE 3rd
Presentation By The Hon. H.E. Talbott

Nashua wins the Belmont Stakes. *Courtesy of the Belair Stable Museum.*

He set a track record in the Preakness. In a match race, Nashua will push Swaps so hard all the way that he will run away from him at the finish."[40]

The media continued to report on a Nashua-Swaps rematch, and it was rumored that the two champions would meet in California. However, Billy Woodward put an end to such rumors when he announced in July that Nashua would not be heading west. Shipping such a long distance would not be in Nashua's best interest. Rather, Swaps and Nashua would meet on neutral ground.

Stories vary widely as to how the meeting ultimately came to fruition. Some say that the race was organized by Billy Woodward immediately following Nashua's Derby loss. Others assert that the match was arranged by actor Don Ameche, who was a friend of both Ellsworth and Woodward. Regardless of its origin, a match race was arranged for August 31, 1955, at Chicago's Washington Park. The winner-take-all matchup, with a hefty purse of $100,000, was referred to as the "match of the century."

Billy Woodward was thrilled with the opportunity to avenge Nashua's Derby loss. While Swaps was shipped to Chicago for training, Team Nashua shipped its colt to Saratoga. Mr. Fitz would later say, "Training in Saratoga makes a horse fit. In a match race the object is to run from the gate, and the fittest horse wins."

The deepness of Saratoga's dirt track proved a perfect training ground for Nashua. Billy himself made a fashionable presence at the Spa, driving through the quaint town in an unusual automobile. Billy's Studillac—a

Maryland governor Samuel Ogle, original master of Belair. *Courtesy of the Belair Stable Museum.*

Left: Colonel Benjamin Tasker Jr., importer of the great Selima. *Courtesy of the Belair Stable Museum.*

Below: The Godolphin Arabian, sire of Selima. *Courtesy of the Library of Congress.*

Portrait of Selima at Belair by William Wilson. *Courtesy of the artist, www.marylandracingart.com.*

Modern view of the Belair Mansion. *Courtesy of Louise Ferro Martin.*

Above: Portrait of Scout II, winner of the Newmarket Stakes. *Courtesy of the Belair Stable Museum.*

Below: Portrait of Granville by Martin Stainforth. *Courtesy of the Belair Stable Museum.*

Above: Modern view of the North Stable. *Courtesy of Louise Ferro Martin.*

Below: Carriage on display at the Stable Museum. *Courtesy of Louise Ferro Martin.*

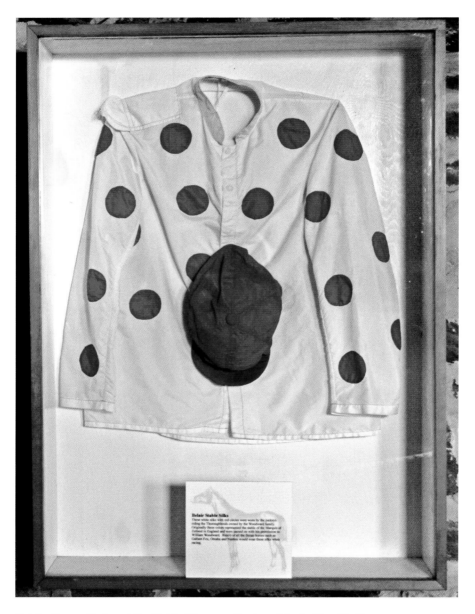

Belair silks on display at the Stable Museum. *Courtesy of Louise Ferro Martin.*

Sign showcasing Belair as the "home of champions." *Courtesy of C. Michael Poole.*

Modern outside view of the stable. *Courtesy of C. Michael Poole.*

Above: Outside view of the Stable Museum. *Courtesy of C. Michael Poole.*

Below: The stable hallway as it appears today. *Courtesy of C. Michael Poole.*

Above: Modern portrait of Gallant Fox by artist Heather Rohde. *Courtesy of the artist (www. rohdefineart.com).*

Left: Gallant Fox's stall sign at the Stable Museum. *Courtesy of Louise Ferro Martin.*

Modern portrait of Omaha by artist Heather Rohde. *Courtesy of the artist (www.rohdefineart.com).*

Above: Tack in the stable museum. *Courtesy of C. Michael Poole.*

Below: Postcard of a portrait of Nashua by W. Smithson Broadhead, commissioned by Billy Woodward. *Courtesy of Cindy Dulay.*

Nashua wins over Summer Tan in the 1955 Wood Memorial. *16″ x 12″ acrylic painting by Theresa Aresco of PhotofinishStudio.com.*

Above: Nashua's grave at Spendthrift Farm. *Courtesy of Cheryl Denton.*

Below: Close-up of Nashua's memorial at Spendthrift by sculptress Liza Todd. *Courtesy of Cheryl Denton.*

Above: Ruler on Ice, winner of the 2011 Belmont Stakes. *Courtesy of Cindy Dulay, horse-races.net.*

Below: Horse of the Year Havre de Grace, winner of the 2011 Woodward Stakes. *Courtesy of Cindy Dulay, horse-races.net.*

Above: Royal Delta, winner of the 2011 Breeders' Cup Ladies' Classic. *Courtesy of Cindy Dulay, horse-races.net.*

Below: Drosselmeyer, winner of the 2011 Breeders' Cup Classic. *Courtesy of Jessie Holmes.*

Billy Woodward (with his wife, Ann, and jockey Eddie Arcaro) accepts Nashua's Belmont Stakes trophy. *Courtesy of the Belair Stable Museum.*

customized hardtop Studebaker with a V-8 Cadillac engine—earned the attention of many, including novelist Ian Fleming, author of the James Bond series. In fact, Billy and his Studillac so impressed Fleming that the author incorporated both into his latest work-in-progress. When the book, *Diamonds Are Forever*, was released the following year, Fleming dedicated it in part to "the memory of w.w. jr. at Saratoga, 1954 and 1955."

With his training at Saratoga completed, Nashua boarded a train bound for Illinois. The media followed the colt's every move, and Nashua was surrounded by eager paparazzi when he arrived at his Chicago destination.

Match races had been popular since the earliest days of racing, and the Nashua-Swaps showdown would be no exception. In the earliest years of U.S. racing, fans had clamored to watch showdowns between two great horses. Key matches included Ten Broeck versus Mollie McCarthy in 1878 at Churchill Downs, a showdown that prompted the creation of a folk song. Since that time, other key matches had included Man o' War versus Sir

Barton and the unforgettable duel between Seabiscuit and War Admiral. The Nashua-Swaps showdown would follow this same pattern, drawing hordes of new, excited fans to the track. *Sports Illustrated* would later write of the race:

> *The match race between Swaps and Nashua provided the biggest racing moment of 1955 and determined the year's top Thoroughbred. Thoroughbreds thundered around U.S. tracks in approximately 31,000 races this year, but the one race that will stand above them all was the $100,000 winner-take-all match race at Chicago's Washington Park. It had all the elements that make for intense drama: the West was represented by Swaps, a golden chestnut unbeaten in eight 1955 starts and victor in the Kentucky Derby. From his home at Aqueduct, to uphold the prestige of the East—and to find revenge for his Derby defeat—came Nashua, the strapping bay. As the pair paraded to the post, they commanded the undivided attention of the racing world and aroused millions of others who do not ordinarily think of themselves as racing fans.*[41]

In an effort to satisfy the crowd's growing fascination with Nashua and Swaps, the two horses would be saddled in an area in front of the stands. In the days prior to the race, the two horses were schooled for saddling in this area. While Swaps appeared unfazed by the commotion, Nashua showed some of his Nasrullah temperament. *Sports Illustrated* wrote:

> *As he walked before the stands in this unusual dress rehearsal for Wednesday's saddling procedure he stopped four times of his own accord. On each occasion, after a hasty survey of his surroundings, Nashua reared back like a frisky, unbroken yearling. Each time, of course, Groom Alfred Robertson got him back to earth but each time, as Robertson said, "He gave me the scare of my life. He was so full of it I thought he might go clear over backwards."*[42]

Despite Nashua's prerace antics, he appeared to warm up well. Prior to the race, Billy's instructions to Arcaro were simple: "Go to the front if possible—but forget the if possible." Arcaro, riding on the inside track, followed Billy's instructions precisely. Expecting that Swaps would take the customary early lead, Arcaro made sure that he and Nashua broke first. Arcaro shouted wildly as the starting box opened, guiding his mount into the section of the track that maintained better, and drier, footing.

Nashua (Eddie Arcaro, up) leads Swaps (Willie Shoemaker, up) around the turn in the match race. *Courtesy of the Keeneland Library.*

Arcaro's thundering voice, juxtaposed with frequent swats from his whip, immediately propelled Nashua into the lead. The big bay would lead wire-to-wire, opening up from an early half-length lead to an ultimate six and a half lengths. Following the victory, Nashua and Arcaro were led by a joyful Billy Woodward to the winner's circle, where a blanket of flowers and a blue ribbon were placed gently onto the colt's neck. The champion of the East had prevailed and had cemented his position as Horse of the Year.

Three weeks after the match race, Nashua took on older horses in the Sysonby Stakes at Belmont, where he placed a disappointing third behind the elder High Gun in what was to be his second Sysonby win. The race had added a $100,000 purse with the hope of attracting both Swaps and Nashua, but Swaps had returned home to California. Swaps, who had battled hoof problems, had apparently re-injured a forefoot in the match race. While some of the media attributed Swaps's performance to this injury, Tenney and Ellsworth asserted that the colt had been sound at the beginning of the race. "If I had an alibi for this race, which I don't," Ellsworth said, "I'd feel a lot better."[43]

Nashua increases his lead over Swaps in the great match race. *Courtesy of the Keeneland Library.*

The match race trophy presentation. Included, from left to right, are jockey Willie Shoemaker, actress Margaret O'Brien, Rex Ellsworth, Eddie Arcaro, Billy and Ann Woodward and Sunny Jim Fitzsimmons. *Courtesy of the Belair Stable Museum.*

Nashua completed his classic season with a win in the Jockey Club Gold Cup over two miles at Belmont. He was then shipped to Aqueduct for a brief respite at Mr. Fitz's stable and was scheduled to spend several weeks at Belair before heading to Florida for the winter. With earnings of $945,415, the Belair colt had become the second leading money winner in racing history to date, trailing only the great Citation. A jubilant Mr. Fitz told *Sports Illustrated*, "If we win 'em all I guess we'll be up around Citation's record somewhere. Sure, I'd like to have the record money-winning horse. It's not so much for the money value, you understand—but I would like to see Mr. Woodward able some day to send a really good horse to stud. His father would have wanted it that way."[44]

Inspired by Nashua's continued success, Billy Woodward had great plans for Belair. In addition to expanding the Thoroughbred program, Billy planned to return Belair to a full working farm, complete with the breeding of shorthorn cattle and Clydesdales and the planting of various crops. In early October 1955, Billy had purchased a Helio, a small four-seater airplane

Belair shorthorn steers. *Courtesy of the Belair Stable Museum.*

that was custom made for him in Kansas. The plane was a new invention, having been recently patented by a professor at the Massachusetts Institute of Technology. Billy's intention was to use the plane to make frequent visits to Belair, the first of which occurred on October 22. Landing on Belair's lush grass in the newly minted Helio, an excited Billy greeted the staff and announced that the great Nashua would be arriving within weeks.

With his visit completed, Billy headed to Claiborne Farm in Kentucky to inspect the latest crop of Belair foals. From there, he directed the Helio to his residence in Oyster Bay Cove, New York, a posh suburb of Long Island. The Woodwards' residence, called "the Playhouse," was situated on sixty acres and had originally belonged to the Woolworth family.

The evening of October 30 was a foggy one and, by 8:30 p.m., the Woodwards' neighborhood was enveloped in a mist of darkness. It was around that time that Ann and Billy hopped into the Studillac and headed for the nearby home of George and Edith Baker. The occasion was a lavish dinner party honoring Wallis Simpson, the duchess of Windsor.

Nashua's team. In the foreground, from left to right, are Sunny Jim Fitzsimmons, Eddie Arcaro and Ann and Billy Woodward. *Courtesy of the Belair Stable Museum.*

Midway through the evening, the chatter at the Baker party focused on the presence of a neighborhood prowler. The gossip caught the attention of both Billy and Ann, who, according to sources, were vividly apprehensive about the situation. Arriving home after midnight at the Playhouse and noting that everything was in its correct place, the couple retreated to their separate bedrooms.

Alarmed by the possibility of an early morning intruder, Billy placed a revolver on his nightstand, while Ann slept beside a double-barreled shotgun. The latter had been a gift from Billy to his wife, who enjoyed hunting tigers while on safari in India. A photo of Ann beside a lifeless tiger was framed and displayed in Ann's bedroom.

Sometime in the wee hours of the morning, Ann Woodward was awakened by the barking of the family dog, Sloppy, and the patter of heavy footsteps on the roof above her bedroom. Arising from her bed and entering the narrow hallway, Ann was startled by the presence of a tall figure outside Billy's bedroom. She shot twice, releasing birdshot into the air and causing what the maid later described as the "sounds of a car backfiring." Upstairs, the children, Woody and Jimmy, slept soundly.

Birdshot soared through the darkened hallway, and the shadowy figure fell to the ground. Examining the naked body of the victim, Ann realized that she had shot her own husband. Billy's lifeless body was lying on the floor; his head was turned to the side, where blood seeped from his cheek and into the carpet. Ann's second shot had ricocheted off the door and struck Billy's face; when he turned his head, perhaps hearing a noise, a pellet had lodged in his brain. Death occurred within ten minutes. At thirty-five years of age, the master of Belair was dead.

Billy had not been carrying a weapon; his gun remained on his bedside table. Realizing what she had done, Ann fell to the ground, and her deep, piercing sobs alerted the night watchman. When the officers arrived at the Woodward residence, Ann admitted that she had accidentally killed her husband, having mistaken him for a prowler.

Billy Woodward's funeral was attended by many and was reported as "the largest since the funeral of Babe Ruth." Flags flew at half-mast at the Hanover Bank, as well as at several prominent clubs, in Billy's honor. A bouquet of carnations and chrysanthemums in the red and white colors of Belair was placed on the casket, and the young master of Belair was buried beside his father at New York's Woodlawn Cemetery.

A distraught Ann Woodward testified in front of a grand jury, which ruled the death of Billy Woodward an accident. The ruling was compounded by testimony from Paul Wirths, a German immigrant who claimed that he had been outside the Woodward home on the night of the killing. Wirth admitted that he had in fact been attempting to rob the house but became startled by the gunshots and immediately left the scene. Much of the evening's tragic events remained a mystery, but for certain, Belair and its Thoroughbred stable would soon feel the impact of those events.

Billy's popularity as the owner of Nashua made his death a leading news story; headlines proclaimed the killing as "the shooting of the century." *Life* magazine displayed on its pages a poignant photo in which a downtrodden Mr. Fitz feeds Nashua a carrot. *Sports Illustrated*, which had planned to honor Billy as its Sportsman of the Year, scrambled to find a replacement; in December, the baseball player Johnny Podres was featured in Billy's place. In the years to come, the killing of Billy Woodward would inspire several books and films, including *The Two Mrs. Grenvilles* by famed novelist Dominick Dunne.

The events that occurred that night at the Playhouse will forever remain shrouded in mystery. Nevertheless, in his brief foray into horse racing, Billy Woodward left a lasting positive impact on the sport. According to the *Washington Post and Times Herald*, "Young Woodward made a hit wherever he appeared in racing...he proved a champion of modesty in the acceptance of victory and graciousness in acknowledging defeat. He became as deeply interested in racing as was his father."[45]

Chapter 13

BELAIR LIVES ON

B illy Woodward's tragic and unexpected death shook the racing world to its core, and the fate of Belair Stud was largely unknown in the months that followed. Woodward's last will and testament had been drawn five years prior, long before Billy had inherited the Belair estate. As such, the decisions pertaining to the future of Belair—including Nashua and the other Belair stock—reverted to the executors and trustees of the will.

In early December 1955, an announcement was made that Nashua and his sixty-one stable mates would be sold in an unprecedented sealed-bid auction. The horses would be divided into three categories: Group A, which included Nashua alone; Group B, which constituted racing stock and yearlings; and Group C, which consisted of broodmares and weanlings. All bidders would be required to submit their offers by December 15 and would enclose a certified check for approximately 10 percent of the offer amount.

The bids received included a letter from twelve-year-old Karen Ann McGuire of New York, who enclosed a drawing of Nashua along with her offer of $24.03. In her letter, Karen promised Nashua "a good home and loveing [sic] care."[46] The trustees were allegedly so touched by the gesture that, while they did not sell Nashua to Karen, they bought the young girl a more appropriate mount.

Nashua was ultimately sold to a syndicate led by Leslie Combs II, master of Spendthrift Farm in Kentucky. Combs's winning offer of $1,251,200 was the highest price ever paid for a racehorse at that time. Nashua would race as a four-year-old under the orange and blue silks of Spendthrift, retaining his core team of Sunny Jim Fitzsimmons and Eddie Arcaro. In his four-year-old debut at Hialeah, a record crowd of forty-two thousand spectators gathered as Nashua won the Widener Handicap and, in doing so, surpassed the million-dollar earnings mark. Later that season, Nashua overtook Citation as the world's all-time leading money winner to date. In the final race of his career, Nashua won a second consecutive Jockey Club Gold Cup, setting a speed record in the process.

Nashua retired to stallion duty at Spendthrift Farm, where he would sire 77 stakes winners. Among these were the mare Shuveee, who duplicated her sire's feat of winning the Jockey Club Gold Cup twice; Bramalea, winner of the Coaching Club American Oaks; Gold Digger, the dam of the great Mr. Prospector; and 1981 Marlboro Cup winner Noble Nashua. Nashua's daughters would produce 122 stakes winners, including Roberto, sire of Dynaformer.

Paired with devoted groom Clem Brooks for more than a quarter-century, Nashua lived to the advanced age of thirty. In 1982, the great champion was euthanized due to the infirmities of old age and was buried on the Spendthrift property. Two years later, a bronze sculpture featuring Brooks and Nashua was unveiled near Spendthrift's stallion barn (which was affectionately dubbed "the Nashua Motel" in deference to the equine superstar). The sculpture was created by Liza Todd, the daughter of screen legend Elizabeth Taylor.

In 1975, the Nashua Stakes, a race for two-year-olds, was instituted at Aqueduct. Over the years, the race has drawn a multitude of successful runners, with key winners including Rockport Harbor and Bluegrass Cat.

Belair's celebrated trainer, Sunny Jim Fitzsimmons, also lived a long and prosperous life. Following Nashua's retirement, Mr. Fitz continued training horses well into his eighties; his résumé after Nashua included Bold Ruler, 1957 Horse of the Year and sire of the immortal Secretariat. Sunny Jim passed away in 1966 at the age of ninety-one and continues to be remembered as one of the greatest trainers in the history of the sport.

While Nashua was standing at stud in Kentucky, the Belair property and its contents were also sold. In August 1957, real estate developer William J. Levitt purchased the estate for $1,750,000. Later that year in October, the contents of the house, which included a variety of paintings and antique furnishings, sold at auction for approximately $30,000.

Levitt, nicknamed "the King of Suburbia" for his immense postwar housing developments, immediately began construction of Belair at Bowie on the vast acreage that had once served as the Belair Stud farm.

Above: Nashua's first time at pasture in 1956. *Courtesy of the Belair Stable Museum.*

Left: Sunny Jim Fitzsimmons in later years. *Courtesy of the Belair Stable Museum.*

Levitt developed the land from 1957 to 1964, with the Belair Mansion serving as his company headquarters. Upon completion of the project, Levitt sold the mansion and a little over five acres of land to the City of Bowie for the price of one dollar, with the provision that the building could only be used for public purposes. In the following years, the mansion housed a variety of public offices, including the local police station and the Bowie City Hall.

Levitt bequeathed the Belair Stable to the city in 1968, and the building was developed into a museum highlighting Belair's contributions to horse racing. The stable includes various displays and artifacts, ranging from the silks, trophies and tack to Gallant Fox's stall sign and Nashua's racing plates. The stable and mansion were added to the National Register of Historic Places in 1973 and 1977, respectively. In the 1980s and early 1990s, the mansion was restored, and it was opened to the public as a museum in 1995. The mansion displays, among other noted artifacts, portions of William Woodward's substantial art collection, including portraits of key Belair horses.

In 1967, Belair's familiar red-and-white polka-dotted silks returned to the racing scene with the arrival of the colt Damascus. The horse was owned by Edith Woodward Bancroft, the eldest child of William and Elsie Woodward, who had inherited the silks upon the death of her brother, Billy. While Edith did not race her colt under the Belair Stud name, she opted to use the silks in homage to her father and brother. Damascus's wins in 1967 included a brilliant twenty-two-length romp in the Travers Stakes and a record-setting performance in the American Derby, which catapulted the colt to superstar status and earned him Horse of the Year honors. One of the highlights of Damascus's career was his brilliant performance in the aptly named Woodward Stakes.

While Damascus represented the definitive ending of Belair's direct association with racing, the Belair Stud continues to have a lasting impact on the sport many decades later. Until its closure, Belair was the oldest continuously operating Thoroughbred farm in the United States. Several of its records are yet to be duplicated, and Gallant Fox and Omaha remain the only father and son to have each won the Triple Crown. In the period from 1923 to 1955, Belair's horses won an astounding number of races, including three Kentucky Derbies, three Preakness Stakes and a record six Belmont Stakes victories. Additionally, five Belair horses—Gallant Fox, Omaha, Granville, Johnstown and Nashua—were inducted into the National Museum of Racing and Hall of Fame.

The bloodlines of Belair's great champions are apparent in today's Thoroughbred runners, many of whom may be traced as far back as Selima. In 2011 alone, several of the sport's grade-one winners were descended from Nashua. These included Drosselmeyer, winner of the Breeders' Cup Classic; Royal Delta, champion of the Ladies' Classic; and 2011 Belmont Stakes champion Ruler On Ice. Horse of the Year Havre de Grace, the game filly who bested males to win the 2011 Woodward Stakes, is also, perhaps fittingly, a descendant of Woodward's immortal Nashua. Incidentally, Finders Key, who recently appeared on the silver screen as the equine lead in the film *War Horse*, is a great-grandson of Nashua through Bramalea.

Centuries after its original founding, thousands of fans travel to Maryland each year to visit the Belair Stable Museum. There, if only for a brief moment, they may be transported back to the glory days of horse racing when glamour and opulence reigned supreme. They may walk the same ground where Omaha trotted freely and gaze into the stall where Gallant Fox once nibbled hay. Behind a brightly painted red-and-white door, they may imagine how the white-blazed stallion must have nickered happily for his grain. They may touch the shoes that were long ago affixed to the hooves of Nashua, his lofty strides thundering as he blazed to a new track record. And, thanks to the efforts of those who preserved this history, they may step back to the time when horse racing was truly the sport of kings—and Belair stood squarely at its highest peak.

OFFSPRING OF SELIMA

Year	Name	Sire	Description	Notes
1754	Ariel	Traveller	Black colt	Popular sire and ancestor of Lexington
1755	Partner	Traveller	Colt	Successful racer and sire of Mark Anthony
1757	Leonidas' Dam	Traveller	Filly	Grand-dam of George Washington's Magnolia
1758	Stella	Othello	Filly	Dam of Primrose and Thistle
1759	Selim	Othello	Bay colt	Greatest racer of the time
1760	Ebony	Othello	Black filly	Ancestress of Boston and Lexington
1761	Bellair I	Traveller	Colt	Unraced
1762	Spadille	Janus	Black colt	Popular sire of quarter horses
1763	Little Juniper	Juniper	Brown colt	
1765	Black Selima	Fearnought	Black filly	Dam of Young Selima

PEDIGREES OF KEY BELAIR HORSES

Pedigree of Gallant Fox

			Flying Fox
		Ajax	Amie
	Teddy		Bay Ronald
		Rondeau	Doremi
Sire: Sir Gallahad			Carbine
		Spearmint	Maid of the Mint
	Plucky Liege		St. Simon
		Concertina	Comic Song
			Domino
		Commando	Emma C.
	Celt		Amphion
		Maid of Erin	Mavourneen
Dam: Marguerite			Bend Or
		Radium	Taia
	Fairy Ray		St. Frusquin
		Seraph	St. Marina

Pedigree of Omaha

Sire: Gallant Fox	Sir Gallahad	Teddy	Ajax
			Rondeau
		Plucky Liege	Spearmint
			Concertina
	Marguerite	Celt	Commando
			Maid of Erin
		Fairy Ray	Radium
			Seraph
Dam: Flambino	Wrack	Robert Le Diable	Ayrshire
			Rose Bay
		Samphire	Isinglass
			Chelandry
	Flambette	Durbar	Rabelais
			Armenia
		La Flambee	Ajax
			Medeah

Pedigree of Granville

Sire: Gallant Fox	Sir Gallahad	Teddy	Ajax
			Rondeau
		Plucky Liege	Spearmint
			Concertina
	Marguerite	Celt	Commando
			Maid of Erin
		Fairy Ray	Radium
			Seraph
Dam: Gravita	Sarmatian	Sardanapale	Prestige
			Emma C.
		Mousse de Bois	Ajax
			Rose Mousse
	Gravitate	Rock View	Rock Sand
			Golden View
		Lady Carnot	Radium
			Gravitation

Pedigree of Johnstown

Sire: Jamestown	Saint James	Ambassador	Dark Ronald
			Excellenza
		Bobolink	Willownyx
			Chelandry
	Mlle. Dazie	Fair Play	Hastings
			Fairy Gold
		Toggery	Rock Sand
			Tea's Over
Dam: La France	Sir Gallahad	Teddy	Ajax
			Rondeaux
		Plucky Liege	Spearmint
			Concertina
	Flambette	Durbar	Rabelais
			Armenia
		La Flambee	Ajax
			Medeah

Pedigree of Nashua

Sire: Nasrullah	Nearco	Pharos	Phalaris
			Scapa Flow
		Nogara	Havresac
			Catnip
	Mumtaz Begum	Blenheim II	Blandford
			Malva
		Mumtaz Mahal	The Tetrarch
			Lady Josephine
Dam: Segula	Johnstown	Jamestown	St. James
			Mlle. Dazie
		La France	Sir Gallahad III
			Flambette
	Sekhmet	Sardanapale	Prestige
			Gemma
		Prosopopee	Sans Souci
			Peroraison

RACING RECORDS OF KEY BELAIR STUD CHAMPIONS

GALLANT FOX'S KEY RACES

Total Racing Record: 17 starts (11 firsts, 3 seconds and 2 thirds)

YEAR	RACE	PLACING
1930	Saratoga Cup	1st
1930	Lawrence Realization Stakes	1st
1930	Jockey Club Gold Cup	1st
1930	Wood Memorial Stakes	1st
1930	Dwyer Stakes	1st
1930	Belmont Stakes	1st
1930	Kentucky Derby	1st
1930	Preakness Stakes	1st
1930	Classic Stakes	1st
1930	Travers Stakes	2nd
1929	Flash Stakes	1st
1929	Junior Champion Stakes	1st
1929	United States Hotel Stakes	2nd
1929	Futurity Stakes	3rd

OMAHA'S KEY RACES

Total Racing Record: 22 starts (9 firsts, 7 seconds and 2 thirds)

YEAR	RACE	PLACING
1936	Ascot Gold Cup	2nd
1936	Princess of Wales's Stakes	2nd
1935	Dwyer Stakes	1st
1935	Belmont Stakes	1st
1935	Preakness Stakes	1st
1935	Classic Stakes	1st
1935	Kentucky Derby	1st
1935	Withers Stakes	2nd
1935	Brooklyn Handicap	3rd
1935	Wood Memorial Stakes	3rd
1934	Champagne Stakes	2nd
1934	Junior Champion Stakes	2nd
1934	Sanford Stakes	2nd

FAIRENO'S KEY RACES

Total Racing Record: 62 starts (17 firsts, 13 seconds and 6 thirds)

YEAR	RACE	PLACING
1935	Saratoga Cup	3rd
1935	Merchants' and Citizens' Handicap	1st
1934	Empire City Handicap	1st
1934	Rochambeau Handicap	1st
1934	Havre de Grace Handicap	1st
1934	Jockey Club Gold Cup	2nd
1934	Saratoga Cup	2nd

Year	Race	Placing
1934	Whitney Gold Trophy Handicap	2nd
1934	Saratoga Handicap	3rd
1934	Wilson Stakes	3rd
1932	Shevlin Stakes	1st
1932	Saratoga Handicap	1st
1932	Lawrence Realization Stakes	1st
1932	Dwyer Stakes	1st
1932	Belmont Stakes	1st
1932	Hawthorne Handicap	1st
1932	Hawthorne Gold Cup	2nd
1931	Consolation Claiming	1st
1931	Junior Champion Stakes	1st
1931	Nursery Handicap	1st
1931	Victoria Stakes	1st
1931	Pimlico Home-Bred	2nd
1931	Suffolk Claiming Stakes	2nd
1931	Troy Claiming Stakes	3rd

Granville's Key Races

Total Racing Record: 18 starts (8 firsts, 4 seconds and 3 thirds)

Year	Race	Placing
1936	Kenner Stakes	1st
1936	Saratoga Cup	1st
1936	Lawrence Realization	1st
1936	Travers Stakes	1st
1936	Belmont Stakes	1st
1936	Arlington Classic Stakes	1st
1936	Suburban Handicap	2nd

Year	Race	Placing
1936	Wood Memorial Stakes	2nd
1936	Preakness Stakes	2nd
1935	Babylon Handicap	3rd
1935	Champagne Stakes	3rd

Fighting Fox's Key Races

Total Racing Record: 35 starts (9 firsts, 7 seconds and 8 thirds)

Year	Race	Placing
1940	Paumonok Handicap	1st
1939	Wilmington Handicap	1st
1939	Fleetwing Handicap	1st
1939	Jamaica Handicap	1st
1939	Carter Handicap	1st
1939	Massachusetts Handicap	1st
1939	Harford Handicap	2nd
1939	Toboggan Handicap	2nd
1939	Excelsior Handicap	2nd
1939	Queens County Handicap	3rd
1938	Wood Memorial Stakes	1st
1938	Kenner Stakes	2nd
1938	Wilson Stakes	2nd
1938	Empire City Handicap	2nd
1938	Whitney Stakes	3rd
1938	Aqueduct Handicap	3rd
1938	Bay Shore Handicap	3rd
1938	Travers Stakes	3rd
1937	Grand Union Hotel Stakes	1st
1937	Junior Champion Stakes	2nd

Year	Race	Placing
1937	Champagne Stakes	3rd
1937	Futurity Stakes	3rd
1937	Hopeful Stakes	3rd

Foxbrough's Key Races

Total Racing Record: 26 starts (5 firsts, 5 seconds and 3 thirds)

Year	Race	Placing
1941	Yonkers Handicap	1st
1941	Butler Handicap	1st
1941	Aqueduct Handicap	2nd
1941	Massachusetts Handicap	2nd
1941	Edgemere Handicap	3rd
1940	Scarsdale Handicap	2nd
1940	Westchester Handicap	2nd
1940	Continental Handicap	3rd

Johnstown's Key Races

Total Racing Record: 21 starts (14 firsts, 0 seconds and 3 thirds)

Year	Race	Placing
1939	Withers Stakes	1st
1939	Paumonok Handicap	1st
1939	Dwyer Stakes	1st
1939	Wood Memorial Stakes	1st
1939	Belmont Stakes	1st
1939	Kentucky Derby	1st
1939	Classic Stakes	3rd
1938	Babylon Handicap	1st

YEAR	RACE	PLACING
1938	Breeders' Futurity	1st
1938	Remsen Handicap	1st
1938	Richard Johnson Stakes	1st
1938	Hopeful Stakes	3rd
1938	Junior Champion Stakes	3rd

VAGRANCY'S KEY RACES

Total Racing Record: 42 starts (15 firsts, 8 seconds and 8 thirds)

YEAR	RACE	PLACING
1943	Diana Handicap	2nd
1943	Ladies' Handicap	2nd
1943	Beldame Handicap	3rd
1943	New York Handicap	3rd
1942	Alabama Stakes	1st
1942	Test Stakes	1st
1942	Gazelle Stakes	1st
1942	Queen Isabella Handicap	1st
1942	Delaware Oaks	1st
1942	Coaching Club American Oaks	1st
1942	Pimlico Oaks	1st
1942	Beldame Handicap	1st
1942	Ladies Handicap	1st
1942	Acorn Stakes	2nd
1942	Lawrence Realization	2nd
1942	New England Oaks	2nd
1941	Selima Stakes	3rd

NASHUA'S KEY RACES

Total Racing Record: 30 starts (22 firsts, 4 seconds and 1 third)

YEAR	RACE	PLACING
1956*	Jockey Club Gold Cup	1st
1956*	Woodward Stakes	2nd
1956*	Monmouth Handicap	1st
1956*	Suburban Handicap	1st
1956*	Camden Handicap	1st
1956*	Grey Lag Handicap	1st
1956*	Widener Handicap	1st
1955	Jockey Club Gold Cup	1st
1955	Sysonby Stakes	3rd
1955	Washington Park Match Race	1st
1955	Arlington Classic	1st
1955	Dwyer Stakes	1st
1955	Belmont Stakes	1st
1955	Preakness Stakes	1st
1955	Kentucky Derby	2nd
1955	Wood Memorial Stakes	1st
1955	Florida Derby	1st
1955	Flamingo Stakes	1st
1954	Futurity Stakes	1st
1954	Cowdin Stakes	2nd
1954	Hopeful Stakes	1st
1954	Grand Union Hotel Stakes	1st
1954	Cherry Hill Stakes	2nd
1954	Juvenile Stakes	1st

*Racing for Spendthrift Farm

WINNERS OF THE SELIMA STAKES

Year	Winner	Age	Jockey	Trainer
2011	Softly Lit	2	Sarah Rook	Dane Kobiskie
2010	*no race*	–	*no race*	*no race*
2009	*no race*	–	*no race*	*no race*
2008	*no race*	–	*no race*	*no race*
2007	Bsharpsonata	2	Eric Camacho	Timothy Salzman
2006	Street Sounds	2	Ramon Dominguez	Michael Matz
2005	J'ray	2	Jerry Bailey	Todd Pletcher
2004	Hear Us Roar	2	Stewart Elliott	Fran Campitelli
2003	Richetta	2	Rick Wilson	Robin Graham
2002	Makin Heat	2	Mark Johnston	Jerry Robb
2001	*no race*	–	*no race*	*no race*
2000	Haitian Vacation	2	Rick Wilson	Eddie Kenneally
1999	Jostle	2	Stewart Elliott	John Servis

WINNERS OF KEY RACES NAMED FOR BELAIR OR ITS HORSES

Owner	Distance (Miles)	Time	Purse	Grade
PTK, LLC	6 fur.	1:14.83	$75,000	
no race	*no race*	*0.00.00*	*no race*	
no race	*no race*	*0.00.00*	*no race*	
no race	*no race*	*0.00.00*	*no race*	
Cloverleaf Farm II	$1^{1}/_{16}$	1:43.66	$100,000	
Hidden Creek Farm	$1^{1}/_{16}$	1:46.35	$100,000	
Lawrence Goichman	$1^{1}/_{16}$	1:41.87	$125,000	
John Davison	$1^{1}/_{16}$	1:46.24	$125,000	
Higgins & Bowman Stable	$1^{1}/_{16}$	1:44.76	$100,000	
Michael Gill	$1^{1}/_{16}$	1:47.60	$100,000	
no race	*no race*	*0.00.00*	*no race*	
Everest Stables	$1^{1}/_{8}$	1:53.81	$100,000	
Fox Hill Farms	$1^{1}/_{8}$	1:52.16	$100,000	III

APPENDIX D

Year	Winner	Age	Jockey	Trainer
1998	Magic Broad	2	Edgar Prado	Richard W. Small
1997	Clark Street	2	Edgar Prado	William Badgett Jr.
1996	Reach the Top	2	Edgar Prado	Mary E. Eppler
1995	River of Rum	2	William McCauley	Richard Schosberg
1994	Stormy Blues	2	Jose A. Santos	Flint S. Schulhofer
1993	Irish Forever	2	Edgar Prado	J. William Boniface
1992	Booly	2	Mike Luzzi	Vincent L. Blengs
1991	Ken de Saron	2	Edgar Prado	Maurice Zilber
1990	Tycoon's Drama	2	Cash Asmussen	Robert Collet
1989	Sweet Roberta	2	Kent Desormeaux	William I. Mott
1988	Capades	2	Angel Cordero Jr.	Richard O'Connell
1987	Minstrel's Lassie	2	Freddy Head	Francois Boutin
1986	Collins	2	George Martens	Flint S. Schulhofer
1985	I'm Splendid	2	Vincent Bracciale Jr.	James J. Toner
1984	Mom's Command	2	Gregg McCarron	Edward T. Allard
1983	Miss Oceana	2	Eddie Maple	Woody Stephens
1982	Bemissed	2	Frank Lovato Jr.	Woody Stephens
1981	Snow Plow	2	Jack Kaenel	Leon Blusiewicz
1980	Heavenly Cause	2	Laffit Pincay Jr.	Woody Stephens
1979	Smart Angle	2	Sam Maple	Woody Stephens

Owner	Distance (Miles)	Time	Purse	Grade
Robert E. Meyerhoff	$1^1/_8$	1:52.60	$100,000	III
Shortleaf Stable	$1^1/_8$	1:56.00	$100,000	III
Samuel Rogers	$1^1/_8$	1:52.40	$100,000	III
R.C. Halvorson	7.5 fur.	1:32.40	$100,000	III
Harriet Finkelstein	7.5 fur.	1:30.20	$100,000	III
Roger Schipke	$1^1/_{16}$	1:48.40	$145,400	III
Sy Cohen	$1^1/_{16}$	1:45.20	$200,000	III
E.M. Fares	$1^1/_{16}$	1:49.80	$200,000	III
R. Strauss/R. Aubert	$1^1/_{16}$	1:44.60	$300,000	III
Diana M. Firestone	$1^1/_{16}$	1:46.00	$300,000	II
Poma Stable	$1^1/_{16}$	1:44.80	$300,000	I
Allen E. Paulson	$1^1/_{16}$	1:45.60	$250,000	I
Frances A. Genter	$1^1/_{16}$	1:43.80	$260,000	I
Caesar P. Kimmel	$1^1/_{16}$	1:43.00	$235,000	I
Peter Fuller	$1^1/_{16}$	1:43.60	$253,000	I
Newstead Farm	$1^1/_{16}$	1:44.00	$215,000	I
Ryehill Farm	$1^1/_{16}$	1:44.00	$227,000	I
Joanne Blusiewicz	$1^1/_{16}$	1:46.20	$210,000	I
Ryehill Farm	$1^1/_{16}$	1:43.40	$160,000	I
Ryehill Farm	$1^1/_{16}$	1:45.20	$170,000	I

Year	Winner	Age	Jockey	Trainer
1978	Candy Éclair	2	Anthony Black	S. Allen King
1977	Lakeville Miss	2	Ruben Hernandez	Jose A. Martin
1976	Sensational	2	Jorge Velasquez	Woody Stephens
1975	Optimistic Gal	2	Darrel McHargue	LeRoy Jolley
1974	Aunt Jin	2	Carlos Marquez	Sonny Hightower
1973	Dancealot	2	Laffit Pincay Jr.	Woody Stephens
1972	La Prevoyante	2	John LeBlanc	Yonnie Starr
1971	Numbered Account	2	Braulio Baeza	Roger Laurin
1970	Patelin	2	Laffit Pincay Jr.	Sylvester Veitch
1969	Predictable	2	Robert Ussery	Edward A. Neloy
1968	Shuvee	2	Ron Turcotte	Willard C. Freeman
1967	Syrian Sea	2	Eddie Belmonte	Casey Hayes
1966	Regal Gleam	2	Manuel Ycaza	Hirsch Jacobs
1965	Moccasin	2	Larry Adams	Harry Trotsek
1964	Marshua	2	Wayne Chambers	Norman R. McLeod
1963	My Card	2	Buck Thornburg	Oscar White
1962	Fool's Play	2	Johnny Sellers	James E. Fitzsimmons
1961	Tamarona	2	Johnny Sellers	Max Hirsch
1960	Good Move	2	Eric Guerin	William C. Winfrey
1959	La Fuerza	2	Sammy Boulmetis	Max Hirsch

Owner	Distance (Miles)	Time	Purse	Grade
Adele W. Paxson	$1^1/_{16}$	1:45.60	$140,000	I
Randolph Weinsier	$1^1/_{16}$	1:45.40	$125,000	I
Mill House Stable	$1^1/_{16}$	1:43.80	$130,000	I
Diana M. Firestone	$1^1/_{16}$	1:42.80	$140,000	I
Paul Cresci	$1^1/_{16}$	1:44.00	$135,000	I
Mill House Stable	$1^1/_{16}$	1:42.80	$125,000	I
Jean-Louis Lévesque	$1^1/_{16}$	1:46.40	$125,000	I
Ogden Phipps	$1^1/_{16}$	1:44.40	$130,000	
George D. Widener Jr.	$1^1/_{16}$	1:45.40	$125,000	
Wheatley Stable	$1^1/_{16}$	1:43.20	$125,000	
Anne Minor Stone	$1^1/_{16}$	1:44.80	$112,500	
Christopher Chenery	$1^1/_{16}$	1:44.40	$112,500	
Patrice Jacobs	$1^1/_{16}$	1:44.80	$130,500	
Claiborne Farm	$1^1/_{16}$	1:45.80	$100,500	
Mrs. W. Gilroy	$1^1/_{16}$	1:44.20	$100,000	
Sarah F. Jeffords	$1^1/_{16}$	1:48.20	$100,000	
Wheatley Stable	$1^1/_{16}$	1:46.80	$60,000	
King Ranch	$1^1/_{16}$	1:45.60	$60,000	
Alfred G. Vanderbilt II	$1^1/_{16}$	1:44.60	$62,000	
King Ranch	$1^1/_{16}$	1:47.80	$65,000	

Year	Winner	Age	Jockey	Trainer
1958	Rich Tradition	2	William Boland	Casey Hayes
1957	Guide Line	2	William Boland	Charlie Whittingham
1956	Lebkuchen	2	Johnny Longden	
1955	Levee	2	Ray Broussard	Norman R. McLeod
1954	High Voltage	2	Ray Broussard	James E. Fitzsimmons
1953	Small Favor	2	Pete McLean	Sylvester Veitch
1952	Tritium	2	Ronnie Nash	Preston M. Burch
1951	Rose Jet	2	Eric Guerin	William Booth
1950	Aunt Jinny	2	Nick Wall	Duval A. Headley
1949	Bed O' Roses	2	Eric Guerin	William C. Winfrey
1948	Gaffery	2	Carson Kirk	Richard E. Handlen
1947	Whirl Some	2	Douglas Dodson	Horace A. Jones
1946	Bee Ann Mac	2	Abelardo DeLara	Max Hirsch
1945	Athene	2	Warren Mehrtens	William J. Hirsch
1944	Busher	2	Eddie Arcaro	James W. Smith
1943	Miss Keeneland	2	Fred A. Smith	Ben A. Jones
1942	Askmenow	2	Carroll Bierman	Kenneth Osborne
1941	Ficklebush	2	Kenneth McCombs	Richard E. Handlen
1940	Valdina Myth	2	Harry Richards	John J. Flanigan

Owner	Distance (Miles)	Time	Purse	Grade
Christopher Chenery	$1^1/_{16}$	1:47.00	$65,000	
Llangollen Farm	$1^1/_{16}$	1:45.60	$75,000	
Dr. Eslie Asbury	$1^1/_{16}$	1:44.40	$80,000	
Vernon G. Cardy	$1^1/_{16}$	1:44.60	$85,000	
Wheatley Stable	$1^1/_{16}$	1:45.00	$90,000	
C.V. Whitney	$1^1/_{16}$	1:46.40	$75,000	
Brookmeade Stable	$1^1/_{16}$	1:46.80	$75,000	
Maine Chance Farm	$1^1/_{16}$	1:47.00	$64,000	
Duval A. Headley	$1^1/_{16}$	1:46.40	$62,000	
Sagamore Farm	$1^1/_{16}$	1:45.80	$70,000	
William duPont Jr.	$1^1/_{16}$	1:46.00	$70,000	
Calumet Farm	$1^1/_{16}$	1:46.40	$70,000	
King Ranch	$1^1/_{16}$	1:50.00	$70,000	
Edward Lasker	$1^1/_{16}$	1:47.40	$56,500	
Edward R. Bradley	$1^1/_{16}$	1:49.60	$45,000	
Calumet Farm	$1^1/_{16}$	1:48.40	$35,000	
Hal Price Headley	$1^1/_{16}$	1:46.80	$36,500	
William duPont Jr.	$1^1/_{16}$	1:47.20	$42,000	
Emerson F. Woodward	1	1:41.40	$40,000	

Year	Winner	Age	Jockey	Trainer
1939	War Beauty	2	Alfred Robertson	John Oliver Keene
1938	Big Hurry	2	Fred A. Smith	William J. Hurley
1937	Jacola	2	Wayne Wright	Selby L. Burch
1936	Talma Dee	2	Alfred Robertson	Robert McGarvey
1935	Split Second	2	Eddie Arcaro	Max Hirsch
1934	Nellie Flag	2	Eddie Arcaro	Bert B. Williams
1933	Jabot	2	Charles Kurtsinger	Thomas J. Healey
1932	Notebook	2	Hank Mills	James E. Fitzsimmons
1931	Laughing Queen	2	J. Bejshak	Bud Stotler
1930	Tambour	2	Louis Schaeffer	Preston M. Burch
1929	Khara	2	L. Fator	John Lowe
1928	Current	2	F. Pool	Jack Baker
1927	Bateau	2	E. Ambrose	Scott P. Harlan
1926	Fair Star	2	Oscar Bourassa	Carl Utz

Owner	Distance (Miles)	Time	Purse	Grade
John Oliver Keene	1	1:41.80	$44,000	
Edward R. Bradley	1	1:41.00	$43,000	
Nancy Carr Friendly	1	1:41.80	$40,700	
Milky Way Farms	1	1:39.40	$37,500	
King Ranch	1	1:39.60	$34,500	
Calumet Farm	1	1:38.00	$37,250	
C.V. Whitney	1	1:40.00	$37,250	
Wheatley Stable	1	1:40.60	$39,750	
William R. Coe	1	1:41.00	$39,000	
Preston M. Burch	1	1:39.80	$43,500	
Rancocas Stable	1	1:39.40	$41,250	
Robert S. Clark	1	1:40.60	$37,250	
Walter M. Jeffords Sr.	1	1:39.20	$40,000	
William duPont Jr.	1	1:40.00	$39,000	

WINNERS OF THE GALLANT FOX HANDICAP

Year	Winner	Age	Jockey	Trainer	Owner	Time
2009	Tiger's Rock	3	David Cohen	Todd Pletcher	Starlight Partners	2:47.34
2008	Delosvientos	5	Eddie Castro	Giuseppe Iadisernia	Giuseppe Iadisernia	2:49.33
2007	Nite Light	3	Mike Luzzi	Todd A. Pletcher	Edward P. Evans	2:47.45
2006	Successful Affair	4	Ramon Dominguez	Gary C. Contessa	Winning Move Stable	2:44.22
2005	Navesink River	4	Mike Luzzi	Todd A. Pletcher	Char-Mari Stable	2:44.96
2004	Tamburello	5	Norberto Arroyo Jr.	Michael Miceli	Michael Miceli	2:43.95
2003	Loving	7	Jose L. Espinoza	Richard E. Dutrow Jr.	Goldfarb, Roach et al.	2:45.08
2002	Coyote Lakes	7	Mike Luzzi	Bruce N. Levine	Roderick J. Valente	2:43.54
2001	Coyote Lakes	7	Chuck C. Lopez	Bruce N. Levine	Roderick J. Valente	2:44.77
2000	Coyote Lakes	7	Mike Luzzi	Bruce N. Levine	Roderick J. Valente	2:45.74
1999	Early Warning	4	Jorge F. Chavez	Todd A. Pletcher	Dogwood Stable	2:42.94
1998	Aavelord	4	Chuck C. Lopez	Bruce N. Levine	Roderick J. Valente	2:46.00
1997	Unreal Turn	5	Chuck C. Lopez	Frank Generazio Jr.	Patricia A. Generazio	2:46.60
1996	Ave's Flag	4	Jorge F. Chavez	Steve Klesaris	McNulty, Omland	2:45.80
1995	Yourmissin-thepoint	4	John Velazquez	Steve Klesaris	Mark Parezo	2:45.20

Year	Winner	Age	Jockey	Trainer	Owner	Time
1994	Serious Spender	3	Jorge F. Chavez	Dominick A. Schettino	John Caputo	2:44.80
1993	Michelle Can Pass	5	Mike E. Smith	John M. DeStefano Jr.	Jay Gee Jay Stable	2:46.00
1992	Michelle Can Pass	4	Aaron Gryder	John M. DeStefano Jr.	Jay Cee Jay Stable	2:45.80
1991	Challenge My Duty	4	Chris Antley	D. Wayne Lukas	William M. Rickman	2:47.00
1990	Power Lunch	3	Craig Perret	D. Wayne Lukas	Calumet Farm	2:47.00
1989	Passing Ships	5	Edgar Prado	Robert P. Klesaris	Gold-N-Oats Stable	2:50.20
1988	Nostalgia's Star	6	Eddie Maple	C.R. McGaughey III	Mary J. Hinds	2:45.60
1987	Soar To The Stars	4	Julie Krone	C.R. McGaughey III	Ogden Mills Phipps	2:43.80
1986	Buckley Boy	4	Michael A. Gonzalez	John J. Tammaro Jr.	George C. Frostad	2:44.20
1985	Jane's Dilemma	4	Jorge Velasquez	J. William Boniface	Robert Meyerhoff	2:48.00
1984	Puntivo	4	Robbie Davis	Edward I. Kelly Sr.	Edward I. Kelly Sr.	2:45.80
1983	Dance Caller	3	Jimmy Miranda	H. Allen Jerkens	Hobeau Farm	2:45.80
1982	Bar Dexter	5	Jeffrey Fell	Lou Mondello	Woodside Stud	2:46.60
1981	Alla Breva	4	Richard Migliore	Philip G. Johnson	Ken Mort Stable	2:43.40

Year	Winner	Age	Jockey	Trainer	Owner	Time
1980	Relaxing	4	Ramon Encinas	Angel Penna Sr.	Ogden Phipps	2:43.40
1979	Identical	4	Eric Beitia	Pancho Martin	Viola Sommer	2:43.60
1978	Wise Philip	5	Angel Cordero Jr.	William Boland	Ruth E. Streit	2:45.20
1977	Cunning Trick	4	Jean Cruguet	William H. Turner Jr.	William T. Pascoe	2:44.20
1976	Frampton Delight	4	Steve Cauthen	Everett W. King	Len Ragozin	2:46.00
1975	Sharp Gary	4	Sandy Hawley	Robert J. Frankel	Edward R. Scharps	2:40.40
1974	Big Spruce	5	Angel Santiago	Victor J. Nickerson	Elmendorf Farm	2:41.60
1973	Big Spruce	4	Angel Santiago	Victor J. Nickerson	Elmendorf Farm	2:42.00
1972	Crafty Khale†	3	Braulio Baeza	Robert L. Dotter	Mrs. Nelson I. Asiel	2:41.00
1971	Hitchcock	5	Ron Turcotte	Pancho Martin	Sigmund Sommer	2:42.80
1970	Hitchcock	4	Eddie Belmonte	Pancho Martin	Sigmund Sommer	2:41.60
1969	Ship Leave	3	Angel Cordero Jr.	Angel Penna Sr.	Gustave Ring	2:42.60
1968	Funny Fellow	3	Braulio Baeza	Edward A. Neloy	Wheatley Stable	2:41.80
1967	Niarkos	7	Eddie Belmonte	John H. Adams	Hasty House Farm	2:43.60
1966	Munden Point	4	John L. Rotz	Ira Hanford	Loren P. Guy	2:42.60
1965	Choker	5	Michael Venezia	H. Allen Jerkens	Hobeau Farm	2:48.00

Year	Winner	Age	Jockey	Trainer	Owner	Time
1964	Smart	5	Eldon Nelson	Henry S. Clark	Christiana Stable	2:42.80
1963	Sunrise Flight	4	Larry Adams	Walter A. Kelley	Little M. Farm	2:43.00
1962	Sensitivo	5	Manuel Ycaza	Arnold N. Winick	Robert F. Bensinger	2:42.20
1961	Polylad	5	Herb Hinojosa	Thomas M. Miles	Mrs. Q.A.S. McKean	2:45.60
1960	Don Poggio	4	Sam Boulmetis Sr.	Robert L. Dotter	Gustave Ring	2:55.80
1959	Bald Eagle	4	Manuel Ycaza	Woody Stephens	Cain Hoy Stable	2:41.00
1958	Admiral Vee	6	Ted Atkinson	H. Allen Jerkens	Edward Seinfeld	2:43.40
1957	Eddie Schmidt	4	Ismael Valenzuela	H. Allen Jerkens	Leroy G. Burns	2:42.40
1956	Summer Tan	4	David Erb	Sherrill W. Ward	Dorothy Firestone Galbreath	2:41.60
1955	Misty Morn	3	Sidney Cole	James E. Fitzsimmons	Wheatley Stable	2:42.40
1954	Social Outcast	4	Ovie Scurlock	William C. Winfrey	Alfred G. Vanderbilt II	2:44.80
1953	Royal Vale	5	Jack Westrope	James E. Ryan	Esther du Pont Weir	1:55.40
1952	Spartan Valor	4	James Stout	Frank Catrone	William G. Hellis Jr.	1:56.20
1951	County Delight	4	Eric Guerin	James E. Ryan	Rokeby Stable	1:57.60
1950	Better Self	5	William Boland	Max Hirsch	King Ranch	1:57.00
1949	Coaltown	4	Steve Brooks	Horace A. Jones	Calumet Farm	1:56.20

Year	Winner	Age	Jockey	Trainer	Owner	Time
1948	Faultless	4	Hedley Woodhouse	Horace A. Jones	Calumet Farm	1:57.20
1947	Stymie	6	Conn McCreary	Max Hirsch	Ethel D. Jacobs	2:42.40
1946	Stymie	5	Basil James	Max Hirsch	Ethel D. Jacobs	2:42.80
1945	Reply Paid	3	Herb Lindberg	George W. Carroll	Mrs. Louis Rabinowitz	2:44.60
1944	Some Chance	5	Albert Snider	B. Frank Christmas	Abram S. Hewitt	2:46.00
1943	Eurasian	3	Herb Lindberg	Sol Rutchick	Havahome Stable	2:48.00
1942	Dark Discovery	4	Warren Mehrtens	Max Hirsch	John A. Bell Jr.	2:44.20
1941	Market Wise	3	Wendell Eads	George W. Carroll	Louis Tufano	2:46.00
1940	Salaminia	3	Don Meade	Duval A. Headley	Hal Price Headley	2:43.60
1939	Isolater	6	James Stout	James E. Fitzsimmons	Belair Stud	2:43.00

† In 1972, Autobiography finished first but was disqualified and set back to second.

Winners of the Vagrancy Handicap

Year	Winner	Age	Jockey	Trainer	Owner	Time
2011	Hilda's Passion	4	Javier Castellano	Todd Pletcher	Starlight Racing/ Glasscock	1:14.81
2010	Hour Glass	4	David Cohen	Todd Pletcher	Mill House	1:16.80
2009	Carolyn's Cat	4	Alan Garcia	Kiaran McLaughlin	Mr. & Mrs. William K. Warren	1:16.34
2008	Looky Yonder	4	Garrett Gomez	Rick Dutrow	Lansdon B. Robbins III	1:17.63
2007	Indian Flare	5	Javier Castellano	Robert J. Frankel	Juddmonte Farms	1:16.44
2006	Dubai Escapade	4	Edgar Prado	Eoin G. Harty	Darley Stable	1:15.39
2005	Sensibly Chic	5	John Velazquez	Timothy Tullock Jr.	Lois S. Nervitt	1:16.31
2004	Bear Fan	5	John Velazquez	Wesley Ward	Peter Fan & W. Ward	1:14.46
2003	Shawklit Mint	4	Richard Migliore	Patrick L. Reynolds	Flatbird Stable	1:15.38
2002	Xtra Heat	4	Harry Vega	John Salzman Sr.	Harry Deitchman et al.	1:16.44
2001	Dat You Miz Blue	4	John Velazquez	James A. Jerkens	Cynthia Knight	1:15.32
2000	Country Hideaway	4	Jerry Bailey	C.R. McGaughey III	Ogden Phipps	1:17.05
1999	Gold Princess †	4	John Velazquez	Gary Sciacca	Windbound Farms	1:16.57
1998	Chip	5	Joe Bravo	Hubert Hine	Carolyn Hine	1:15.69
1997	Inquisitive Look	4	Jorge Chavez	Richard Stoklosa	Iselin Kaufman et al.	1:22.07

Year	Winner	Age	Jockey	Trainer	Owner	Time
1996	Twist Afleet	5	Julie Krone	John C. Kimmel	Lucille Conover	1:20.94
1995	Sky Beauty	5	Mike E. Smith	H. Allen Jerkens	Georgia E. Hofmann	1:21.56
1994	Sky Beauty	4	Mike E. Smith	H. Allen Jerkens	Georgia E. Hofmann	1:21.67
1993	Spinning Round	4	Jorge Chavez	Carl J. Domino	Kinsman Stable	1:24.52
1992	Nannerl	5	Jose A. Santos	Scotty Schulhofer	Marablue Farm	1:22.55
1991	Queena	5	Mike E. Smith	C.R. McGaughey III	Emory A. Hamilton	1:22.00
1990	Mistaurian	4	Herb McCauley	Stephen L. DiMauro	Bernard Chaus	1:25.20
1989	Aptostar	4	Angel Cordero Jr.	H. Allen Jerkens	Centennial Farms	1:22.80
1988	Grecian Flight	4	Craig Perret	Joseph Pierce Jr.	Henry Lindh	1:20.80
1987	North Sider	5	Angel Cordero Jr.	D. Wayne Lukas	Eugene V. Klein	1:24.20
1986	Le Slew	4	Jose Santos	D. Wayne Lukas	Eugene V. Klein	1:23.80
1985	Nany	5	Jorge Velasquez	Richard Root	Harry Mangurian Jr.	1:23.80
1984	Grateful Friend	4	Angel Cordero Jr.	Pancho Martin	Harbor View Farm	1:24.00
1983	Broom Dance	4	Gregg McCarron	James W. Maloney	Christiana Stables	1:22.80
1982	Westport Native	4	Jorge Velasquez	Howard Tesher	Oak Cliff Stable	1:22.60
1981	Island Charm	4	Richard Migliore	Stephen A. DiMauro	David McKibbin	1:23.60

Year	Winner	Age	Jockey	Trainer	Owner	Time
1980	Lady Lonsdale	5	Larry Saumell	Vincent Nocella	Pic Stable	1:24.40
1979	Frosty Skater	4	Don MacBeth	Lawrence Jennings	Arthur I. Appleton	1:23.20
1978	Dainty Dotsie	4	Billy Woodward	James Cowden Jr.	James R. Cowden Sr.	1:21.80
1977	Shy Dawn	6	Angel Cordero Jr.	Woodrow Sedlacek	Jacques Wimpfheimer	1:23.80
1976	My Juliet	4	Jorge Velasquez	Eugene Euster	George Weasel Jr.	1:22.00
1975	Honorable Miss	5	Jacinto Vasquez	Frank Y. Whiteley Jr.	Pen-Y-Bryn Farm	1:22.20
1974	Coraggioso	4	Don Brumfield	Anthony Basile	Bwamazon Farm	1:22.40
1973	Krislin	4	Marco Castaneda	Stephen A. DiMauro	Harold Snyder	1:22.60
1972	Chou Croute	4	Robert Kotenko	Robert G. Dunham	E.V. Benjamin III	1:22.40
1971	Golden Or	5	John L. Rotz	Budd Lepman	Crown Stable	1:23.00
1970	Process Shot	3	Chuck Baltazar	J. Bowes Bond	Elberon Farm	1:23.80
1969	Grey Slacks	4	Eddie Belmonte	H. Allen Jerkens	Hobeau Farm	1:23.00
1968	Mac's Sparkler	6	William Boland	H. Allen Jerkens	Hobeau Farm	1:22.60
1967	Triple Brook	5	Braulio Baeza	A. Ridgely White	Norman P. Bate	1:23.80
1966	Queen Empress	4	Braulio Baeza	Edward A. Neloy	Wheatley Stable	1:23.00
1965	Affectionately	5	Walter Blum	Hirsch Jacobs	Ethel D. Jacobs	1:23.00
1964	No Resisting	4	John L. Rotz	Edward A. Neloy	Wheatley Stable	1:23.80

Year	Winner	Age	Jockey	Trainer	Owner	Time
1963	Cicada	4	Larry Adams	Casey Hayes	Meadow Stable	1:22.80
1962	Rose O'Neill	4	Manuel Ycaza	Ted Saladin	Bert W. Martin	1:23.60
1961	Sun Glint	4	S. Cole	Horace A. Jones	Calumet Farm	1:23.60
1960	Mommy Dear	4	William Boland	Eddie Hayward	Circle M Farm	1:22.60
1959	Dandy Blitzen	4	Phil I. Grimm	W. Larue	B.A. Dario	1:22.60
1958	Outer Space	4	Eldon Nelson	James W. Maloney	Mrs. Gerard S. Smith	1:23.80
1957	Plotter	4	Pete Anderson	William Post	Harry La Montagne	1:24.20
1956	Miz Clementine	5	Eddie Arcaro	Horace A. Jones	Calumet Farm	1:23.40
1955	Searching*	3	Conn McCreary	Hirsch Jacobs	Ethel D. Jacobs	1:23.60
1955	Talora*	4	Henry Moreno	Casey Hayes	Meadow Stable	1:24.60
1954	Canadiana	4	Charles O'Brien	Gordon J. McCann	E.P. Taylor	1:23.40
1953	Home-Made	3	Eric Guerin	William C. Winfrey	Alfred G. Vanderbilt II	1:24.60
1952	Marta	5	Conn McCreary	Woody Stephens	Woodvale Farm	1:45.00
1948	Conniver	4	Ted Atkinson	William Post	Harry La Montagne	1:43.60

† In 1999, Hurricane Bertie finished first but was disqualified and set back to second.
*The race was run in two divisions in 1955.

WINNERS OF THE WOODWARD STAKES

Year	Winner	Age	Jockey	Trainer	Owner	Time
2011	Havre de Grace ‡	4	Ramon A. Dominguez	J. Larry Jones	Rick Porter	1:49.18
2010	Quality Road	4	John Velazquez	Todd Pletcher	Edward P. Evans	1:50.00
2009	Rachel Alexandra ‡	3	Calvin Borel	Steve Asmussen	Stonestreet Stables	1:48.29
2008	Curlin	4	Robby Albarado	Steve Asmussen	Stonestreet Stables	1:49.34
2007	Lawyer Ron	4	John Velazquez	Todd Pletcher	Hines Racing, LLC	1:48.60
2006	Premium Tap	4	Kent Desormeaux	John C. Kimmel	Kline, Alevizos, Whelihan	1:50.65
2005	Saint Liam	5	Jerry D. Bailey	Richard E. Dutrow Jr.	William K. Warren Jr.	1:49.07
2004	Ghostzapper	4	Javier Castellano	Robert J. Frankel	Stronach Stables	1:46.20
2003	Mineshaft	4	Robby Albarado	Neil J. Howard	Farish, Elkins, Webber	1:46.20
2002	Lido Palace	5	Jorge F. Chavez	Robert J. Frankel	Amerman Racing Stable	1:47.60
2001	Lido Palace	4	Jerry D. Bailey	Robert J. Frankel	John W. Amerman	1:47.40
2000	Lemon Drop Kid	4	Edgar Prado	Scotty Schulhofer	Jeanne G. Vance	1:50.40
1999	River Keen	7	Chris Antley	Bob Baffert	Hugo Reynolds	1:46.80
1998	Skip Away	5	Jerry D. Bailey	Sonny Hine	Carolyn H. Hine	1:47.80
1997	Formal Gold	4	Kent Desormeaux	William W. Perry	John D. Murphy	1:47.40

Year	Winner	Age	Jockey	Trainer	Owner	Time
1996	Cigar	6	Jerry D. Bailey	William I. Mott	Allen E. Paulson	1:47.00
1995	Cigar	5	Jerry D. Bailey	William I. Mott	Allen E. Paulson	1:47.00
1994	Holy Bull	3	Mike E. Smith	Warren A. Croll Jr.	Warren A. Croll Jr.	1:46.80
1993	Bertrando	4	Gary Stevens	Robert J. Frankel	Edward Nahem/505 Farms	1:47.00
1992	Sultry Song	4	Jerry D. Bailey	Patrick J. Kelly	Live Oak Plantation Racing	1:47.00
1991	In Excess	4	Gary Stevens	Bruce L. Jackson	Jack J. Munari	1:46.20
1990	Dispersal	4	Chris Antley	Grover G. Delp	Tom Meyerhoff	1:45.80
1989	Easy Goer	3	Pat Day	Shug McGaughey	Ogden Phipps	2:01.00
1988	Alysheba	4	Chris McCarron	Jack Van Berg	Dorothy Scharbauer	1:59.40
1987	Polish Navy	3	Randy Romero	Shug McGaughey	Ogden Phipps	1:47.00
1986	Precisionist	5	Chris McCarron	Ross Fenstermaker	Fred W. Hooper	1:46.00
1985	Track Barron	4	Angel Cordero Jr.	LeRoy Jolley	Peter M. Brant	1:46.60
1984	Slew o' Gold	4	Angel Cordero Jr.	John O. Hertler	Equusequity Stable	1:47.80
1983	Slew o' Gold	3	Angel Cordero Jr.	Sidney Watters Jr.	Equusequity Stable	1:46.60
1982	Island Whirl	4	Angel Cordero Jr.	D. Wayne Lukas	Elcee-H Stable	1:46.80
1981	Pleasant Colony	3	Angel Cordero Jr.	John P. Campo	Buckland Farm	1:47.20

Year	Winner	Age	Jockey	Trainer	Owner	Time
1980	Spectacular Bid	4	Bill Shoemaker	Grover G. Delp	Hawksworth Farm	2:02.40
1979	Affirmed	4	Laffit Pincay Jr.	Lazaro S. Barrera	Harbor View Farm	2:01.60
1978	Seattle Slew	4	Angel Cordero Jr.	Douglas Peterson	Tayhill Stable	2:00.00
1977	Forego	7	Bill Shoemaker	Frank Y. Whiteley Jr.	Lazy F Ranch	1:48.00
1976	Forego	6	Bill Shoemaker	Frank Y. Whiteley Jr.	Lazy F Ranch	1:45.80
1975	Forego	5	Heliodoro Gustines	Sherrill W. Ward	Lazy F Ranch	2:27.20
1974	Forego	4	Heliodoro Gustines	Sherrill W. Ward	Lazy F Ranch	2:27.40
1973	Prove Out	4	Jorge Velasquez	H. Allen Jerkens	Hobeau Farm	2:25.80
1972	Key to the Mint †	3	Braulio Baeza	J. Elliott Burch	Rokeby Stable	2:28.40
1971	West Coast Scout	3	John L. Rotz	Mervin Marks	Oxford Stable	2:00.40
1970	Personality	3	Eddie Belmonte	John W. Jacobs	Ethel D. Jacobs	2:01.80
1969	Arts and Letters	3	Braulio Baeza	J. Elliott Burch	Rokeby Stable	2:01.00
1968	Mr. Right	5	Heliodoro Gustines	Evan S. Jackson	Cheray Duchin	2:03.00
1967	Damascus	3	Bill Shoemaker	Frank Y. Whiteley Jr.	Edith W. Bancroft	2:00.60
1966	Buckpasser	3	Braulio Baeza	Edward A. Neloy	Ogden Phipps	2:02.80
1965	Roman Brother	4	Braulio Baeza	Burley Parke	Harbor View Farm	2:01.80
1964	Gun Bow	4	Walter Blum	Edward A. Neloy	Gedney Farm	2:02.40

Year	Winner	Age	Jockey	Trainer	Owner	Time
1963	Kelso	6	Ismael Valenzuela	Carl Hanford	Bohemia Stable	2:00.80
1962	Kelso	5	Ismael Valenzuela	Carl Hanford	Bohemia Stable	2:03.20
1961	Kelso	4	Eddie Arcaro	Carl Hanford	Bohemia Stable	2:00.00
1960	Sword Dancer	4	Eddie Arcaro	J. Elliott Burch	Brookmeade Stable	2:01.20
1959	Sword Dancer	3	Eddie Arcaro	J. Elliott Burch	Brookmeade Stable	2:04.40
1958	Clem	4	Bill Shoemaker	William W. Stephens	Adele L. Rand	2:01.00
1957	Dedicate	5	Bill Hartack	G. Carey Winfrey	Jan Burke	2:01.00
1956	Mister Gus	5	Ismael Valenzuela	Charlie Whittingham	Gustave Ring	2:03.00
1955	Traffic Judge	3	Eddie Arcaro	Woody Stephens	Clifford Mooers	1:48.20
1954	Pet Bully	6	Bill Hartack	Tommy Kelly	Ada L. Rice	1:35.60

‡ designates that a filly or mare won the race
† Cougar II finished first but was disqualified and placed third.

Winners of the Nashua Stakes

Year	Winner	Jockey	Trainer	Owner	Time
2011	Vexor	David Cohen	John Kimmel	Goldmark Farm	1:10.71
2010	To Honor and Serve	Jose Lezcano	William I. Mott	Live Oak Plantation	1:35.86
2009	Buddy's Saint	Jose Lezcano	Bruce Levine	Kingfield Stables	1:35.67
2008	Break Water Edison	Alan Garcia	John Kimmel	Eli Gindi	1:35.86
2007	Etched	Alan Garcia	Kiaran McLaughlin	Darley Stable	1:36.96
2006	Day Pass	John R. Velazquez	Kiaran McLaughlin	Darley Stable	1:36.09
2005	Bluegrass Cat	John R. Velazquez	Todd A. Pletcher	WinStar Farm	1:38.02
2004	Rockport Harbor	Stewart Elliott	John Servis	Fox Hill Farms Inc.	1:36.60
2003	Read the Footnotes	Jerry D. Bailey	Richard Violette Jr.	Klaravich Stables	1:36.40
2002	Added Edge	Patrick Husbands	Mark Casse	Team Valor	1:36.60
2001	Listen Here	Jerry D. Bailey	William I. Mott	Kim Nardelli	1:37.60
2000	Ommadon	Aaron Gryder	Thomas M. Walsh	Sorin Stables	1:36.60
1999	Mass Market	Mike E. Smith	Ben W. Perkins Jr.	New Farm	1:38.60
1998	Doneraile Court	Jerry D. Bailey	Nicholas P. Zito	M. Tabor/J. Magnier	1:36.00
1997	Coronado's Quest	Mike E. Smith	C.R. McGaughey III	Stuart S. Janney III	1:37.00
1996	Jules	Jose Santos	Alan E. Goldberg	Jayeff B. Stables	1:36.80

Year	Winner	Jockey	Trainer	Owner	Time
1995	*no race*	*no race*	*no race*	*no race*	*0.00.0*
1994	Devious Course	Frank Alvarado	H. James Bond	Rudlein Stable	1:37.40
1993	Popol's Gold	Herb McCauley	William H. Turner Jr.	Stephen Stavrides	1:46.60
1992	Dalhart	Mike E. Smith	Thomas Bohannan	Loblolly Stable	1:44.40
1991	Pine Bluff	Craig Perret	Thomas Bohannan	Loblolly Stable	1:46.00
1990	Kyle's Our Man	Jerry D. Bailey	John M. Veitch	Darby Dan Farm	1:45.40
1989	Champagne-forashley	Jacinto Vasquez	Howard M. Tesher	Lions Head Farm	1:45.20
1988	Traskwood	Angel Cordero Jr.	George R. Arnold II	Loblolly Stable	1:45.20
1987	Cougarized	Jose Santos	D. Wayne Lukas	Lloyd R. French Jr.	1:46.00
1986	Bold Summit	Chris Antley	Richard E. Dutrow Jr.	Alvin J. Akman	1:45.00
1985	Raja's Revenge	Robbie Davis	Frank LaBoccetta	Edward Anchel	1:44.40
1984	Stone White	Robbie Davis	Gilbert Puentes	Gilbert Puentes	1:38.20
1983	Don Rickles	Angel Cordero Jr.	John Parisella	Theodore M. Sabarese	1:38.40
1982	I Enclose	Ruben Hernandez	Edward I. Kelly	Brookfield Farms	1:37.60
1981	Our Escapade	Don MacBeth	Roger Laurin	Reginald N. Webster	1:36.80
1980	A Run	Chris McCarron	Larry S. Barrera	Arron U. Jones	1:37.20
1979	Googoplex	Laffit Pincay Jr.	Pancho Martin	Robert N. Lehmann	1:36.40
1978	Instrument Landing	Jeffrey Fell	David A. Whiteley	Pen-Y-Bryn Farm	1:37.00

Year	Winner	Jockey	Trainer	Owner	Time
1977	Quadratic	Eddie Maple	Woody Stephens	August Belmont IV	1:35.40
1976	Nearly On Time	Jacinto Vazquez	Leroy Jolley	Mrs. Moody Jolley	1:35.60
1975	Lord Henribee	Eddie Maple	William H. Turner Jr.	Milton Ritzenberg	1:35.60

NOTES

CHAPTER 1

1. Bulle Rock was the first English Thoroughbred to be imported to the United States in an effort to improve the American breed.
2. Shirley Vlasak Baltz, *Belair from the Beginning* (Bowie, MD: Bowie Heritage Committee, 2005).
3. Ibid., 14–19.

CHAPTER 2

4. Fairfax Harrison, *The Belair Stud* (VA: Old Dominion Press, 1929).
5. C.M. Prior, *The Royal Studs of the Sixteenth and Seventeenth Centuries* (UK: Horse and Hound Publications, 1935).
6. John Eisenberg, "Off to the Races," *Smithsonian* magazine, August 2004.
7. John Hervey, *Racing in America 1665–1865* (New York: Sagamore Press, 1944).

CHAPTER 3

8. Baltz, *Belair from the Beginning*.
9. *Maryland Gazette*, April 1761.
10. Ibid.
11. Ibid.
12. Baltz, *Belair from the Beginning*, 107.

CHAPTER 4

13. *New York Times*, "James T. Woodward, the Banker, Is Dead," April 11, 1910, 1.
14. Ibid.
15. Edward L. Bowen, *Dynasties: Great Thoroughbred Stallions* (KY: Eclipse Press, 2000).
16. Ibid.

CHAPTER 5

17. Ibid.
18. Ibid.
19. Ibid.
20. Ibid.
21. *New York Times*, October 11, 1916.
22. Ibid.

CHAPTER 6

23. Baltz, *Belair from the Beginning*.
24. Anne Peters, "Sir Gallahad," www.tbheritage.com/Portraits/SirGallahad.html.

CHAPTER 7

25. Jimmy Breslin, *Sunny Jim: The Life of America's Most Beloved Horseman* (New York: Doubleday, 1962).
26. *New York Times*, May 1930.
27. *Pittsburgh Press*, May 30, 1930.
28. Bryan Field, "Gallant Fox Beats Whichone 4 Lengths in $81,340 Belmont," *New York Times*, June 8, 1930, 147.
29. *National Turf Digest*, September 1930, 917.

CHAPTER 8

30. *The Blood-Horse*, June 15, 1935.
31. John Hervey, *American Race Horses of 1936* (New York: Sagamore Press, 1937).
32. Journal of Kentucky History and Genealogy, jkhg.org.

Notes

33. Daily Racing Form, referenced in www.spiletta.com/UTHOF/omaha.
html.

Chapter 9

34. "Scarlet Spots," *Time* magazine, August 1939.

Chapter 10

35. Susan Braudy, *This Crazy Thing Called Love* (New York: St Martin's, 1993).
36. Baltz, *Belair from the Beginning*.

Chapter 11

37. *Sports Illustrated*, May 2, 1955.
38. Ibid., September 12, 1955.
39. Ibid.

Chapter 12

40. *Sports Illustrated*, July 18, 1955.
41. Ibid.
42. Ibid.
43. Ibid.
44. *Sports Illustrated*, September 12, 1955.
45. *Washington Post and Times Herald*, November 1, 1955.

Chapter 13

46. *Sarasota Journal*, December 20, 1955.

INDEX

A

Aile d'Or 34
Aqueduct 47, 49, 50, 55, 59, 60, 61,
     67, 75, 84, 87, 95, 98, 101, 106
Arcaro, Eddie 60, 85, 86, 87, 90, 92,
     98, 106
Atkinson, Ted 90

B

Beasley, Pat 77
Belair silks 32, 52, 55, 67, 78, 95
Belmont Stakes 30, 51, 55, 59, 61, 67,
     95, 109
Black Tarquin 75, 77
Boswell 77
Boyd-Rochfort, Cecil 47, 63, 76, 77,
     81, 84
Brooks, Clem 106
Brown Betty 75
Bulle Rock 12
Byrd, William 17

C

Challedon 44, 72, 73
Citation 84, 85, 86, 101, 106
Claiborne Farm 39, 47, 58, 59, 64, 67,
     70, 72, 73, 78, 102

D

Damascus 108

E

Ellsworth, Rex 91, 93, 96, 99
Epsom Derby 30, 51, 59, 65, 70, 77, 81

F

Faireno 67
Fighting Fox 70, 72
Fitzsimmons, Jim 42, 47, 49, 50, 67,
     82, 85, 87, 90, 91, 92, 96, 101,
     104, 106

Flambino 36, 59
Flares 77
Fleming, Ian 97
Foxbrough 70
Foxhall 18, 77

G

Gallant Fox 47, 59, 61, 65, 67, 68, 70,
    108, 109
Godolphin Arabian 15
Gold Digger 106
Granville 68, 108
Groton School 28, 79, 84

H

Hancock, Arthur 45, 47, 59, 72, 82
Hanover Bank 25, 26, 32, 34, 35, 79,
    103
Harvard 28, 31, 79
Hialeah 89, 106
Hopeful Stakes 59, 61, 87
Horse of the Year 62, 68, 70, 99, 106,
    108
Hycilla 77

J

Jackson, Andrew 27, 34, 75
Jamaica 51, 58, 68, 70, 90
Jim Dandy 57
Johnstown 72, 84, 108

K

Kentucky Derby 30, 54, 60, 67, 68, 72,
    90, 92

L

Lawrence Realization 57, 68, 70, 73

M

Man o' War 36, 55, 62, 67, 73, 87, 97
Marguerite 39, 40, 44, 47
match race 93, 97
Mr. Prospector 106

N

Nashua 82, 85, 89, 95, 104, 105, 108,
    109
Nashua River 84
Nasrullah 82, 98
Newmarket 16, 31, 47, 64, 75, 76, 77
Noble Nashua 106

O

Ogle, Benjamin 21, 22, 23
Ogle, Samuel 11, 15
Omaha 59, 67, 68, 77, 108, 109
Othello 21, 23

P

Preakness 33, 52, 61, 67, 68, 73, 93, 95
Prince Simon 81

Q

Queen Mab 13

S

Sande, Earl 51, 52, 55
Saratoga 31, 32, 33, 39, 47, 50, 51, 55,
    56, 57, 59, 62, 68, 70, 82, 87,
    96, 97
Saunders, Willie 60, 61
Seabiscuit 61, 98
Selim 21, 23
Selima 15, 16, 17, 19, 21, 22, 23, 109
Shuvee 106
Sir Gallahad 43, 44, 47, 72, 73, 75,
    77
Spark 13
Stout, James 68, 72
Summer Tan 87, 91, 92
Swaps 91, 93, 95, 99

T

Tasker, Anne 12
Tasker, Benjamin, Jr. 15, 17, 18, 21
Tasker, Benjamin, Sr. 12, 22
Tayloe, John, II 17
Travers Stakes 40, 55, 57, 70, 108
Triple Crown 55, 60, 61, 62, 63, 64,
    65, 108
Tryal 17

V

Vagrancy 73

W

Washington, George 22
Washington Park 96, 98
Whichone 50, 55, 56
White House 40

Wood Memorial 51, 52, 60, 68, 70,
    72, 90
Woodward, Ann 81, 103
Woodward, Billy 38, 78, 81, 82, 84, 85,
    88, 89, 90, 92, 93, 96, 98, 99,
    101, 102, 103, 104, 105, 108
Woodward, Elsie 32, 82
Woodward, James 24, 25, 26, 28, 32,
    34
Woodward Stakes 84, 108, 109
Woodward, William 28, 31, 32, 33, 35,
    38, 39, 47, 50, 51, 54, 58, 61,
    65, 67, 75, 77, 78, 81, 82, 84

ABOUT THE AUTHOR

Kimberly Gatto is a professional writer specializing in equestrian and sports-related books. Her published works to date include two horse-related titles, histories of Churchill Downs and Saratoga Race Course and several athlete biographies. Kim's work has been included in various publications, including the *Blood Horse*, the *Chronicle of the Horse*, the *Equine Journal* and *Chicken Soup for the Horse Lover's Soul*. Gatto is an honors graduate of Boston Latin School and Wheaton College in Massachusetts. A lifelong rider and horsewoman, she is the proud owner of a lovely off-the-track Thoroughbred.